BEATING ASIA'S
NEXT BIG ONE

TSUNAMI ALERT

BEATING ASIA'S NEXT BIG ONE

OAKLEY BROOKS

Marshall Cavendish
Editions

Cover design by OpalWorks Co Ltd
Map illustrations by Benson Tan

© 2010 Nanyang Technological University, Oakley Brooks and Marshall Cavendish International (Asia) Pte Ltd

Published by Marshall Cavendish Editions
An imprint of Marshall Cavendish International
1 New Industrial Road, Singapore 536196

Other Marshall Cavendish Offices

Marshall Cavendish Ltd. PO Box 65829, London EC1P 1NY, UK • Marshall Cavendish Corporation. 99 White Plains Road, Tarrytown NY 10591-9001, USA • Marshall Cavendish International (Thailand) Co Ltd. 253 Asoke, 12th Flr, Sukhumvit 21 Road, Klongtoey Nua, Wattana, Bangkok 10110, Thailand • Marshall Cavendish (Malaysia) Sdn Bhd, Times Subang, Lot 46, Subang Hi-Tech Industrial Park, Batu Tiga, 40000 Shah Alam, Selangor Darul Ehsan, Malaysia

Marshall Cavendish is a trademark of Times Publishing Limited

National Library Board, Singapore Cataloguing-in-Publication Data

Brooks, Oakley.
Tsunami alert : beating Asia's next big one / by Oakley Brooks. – Singapore : Marshall Cavendish Editions, 2010.
p. cm.
ISBN : 978 981 4302 20 3
1. Tsunami Warning System – Asia. 2. Tsunamis – Asia. I. Title.

GC223
551.4637095 -- dc22   OCN669739781

Printed in Singapore by Fabulous Printers Pte Ltd

For H. M. H.
Your patient, warm curiosity led us to this.

Contents

Acknowledgements

L ike any book, this has been the product of many minds, not just one. I can't mention everybody who influenced it and helped it along, but I'll try to hit as many as possible.

At the head of the pack is Kerry Sieh and the group at the Earth Observatory of Singapore. Full of ideas, he shared his journey openly, gave a gentle but unmistakable push whenever the book stalled out, and sparred gamely over a few passages he didn't agree with. I think the results are way better for all of that.

In the publishing realm, Violet Phoon and Chris Newson were both optimists and together they've helped bring the project to fruition. The hardworking team of Stephanie Yeo and Melvin Neo carried the piece adroitly from manuscript to the finish.

I also owe much to Betsy Lerner and her counsel on the book from the moment it was just a seed.

Back at EOS, Sharmini Blok offered moral and logistical support and general good cheer throughout the process and the project wouldn't have worked without her. I'm also grateful for

Pungky Utami and the quiet, gracious conscience of Indonesia she brought, as my neighbor. Hon Sang Liow kept things light, even when I brooded over the screen. Mariton Bornas kept us eating, as only a vivacious Filipina grandma can. A hearty thanks too, to the caring Marie Hamidah, the jolly professor Kusno Megawati, the irrepressible Paramesh Banerjee, the eager French athlete Alex Baguet, the warm southerner Ken MacPherson, the wise Chris Newhall, Christina Widiwijayanti, Dann Hidayat and all the trusty souls in Finance and HR and the Director's office.

Among EOS associates and collaborators, Danny Natawidjaja was liberal with his time and expertise about Sumatran seismology and the issues people faced there. Aron Meltzner, Belle Philibosian and Yu Wang were nurturing with the science and are worthy carriers of the coral code. Brian Atwater squeezed invaluable conversations and readings into his busy schedule. Kenji Satake lent an expert hand, Kate Donovan shared her spot on reading list, and Bambang Suwargadi helped logistically.

In Sumatra, I'm indebted to Patra Dewi for spending so much time explaining Kogami's past, present and future. Febrin Ismail found moments for me too, even though he was trying to run an engineering department, prepare a province and then rebuild a city after the 2009 earthquake. I'm grateful for conversations in the same vein with Matt George, David Lupo, Christina Fowler and Chris Scurrah.

Among countless conversations large and small in Padang, the ones with Aim Zein always seemed to cut to the quick. Time spent with Buya Abidin shed rays of insight.

Tom Plummer and Kirk Willcox first set me up to visit SurfAid's work in the Mentawai Islands after the September 2007 earthquakes and Tom has continued to give me the honest lay of the land in the islands ever since — many thanks.

Koen Meyers has long labored to bridge the gap between science, modernity and indigenous cultures, and yet still managed to unselfishly help me, the newcomer, understand what was at stake in the Mentawais and elsewhere. I'm also grateful to Jose Borrero for giving me a layman's take on tsunami scenarios, to Vasily Titov for sharing a global perspective on tsunami modeling, to Jorn Behrens for laying out the German tsunami model project and to Harald Spahn for explaining the wider tsunami warning system in great detail.

In Padang, I would still be circling in a foreign haze without the wise guidance of Masni Fanshuri, Nafitri Darmali and Jeffri Adriyanto — three trusty translators. The gang at Hotel Padang always made a home for me there. And the late great Hotel Batang Arau café group was always full of uplifting cheer.

Among journalist and writer colleagues, high fives to Tim Sullivan who picked through an early jumble of a draft with utmost care, and the refreshingly blunt Dave Wolman who told me where exactly he got hung up in the weeds. Chuck Colmore gave me hope in the avid reader. Big Oaks Brooks offered up his own worthy critique in the early going. Eric Blokland was the ultimate fact-check/proofread closer to have coming out of the bullpen.

There are quite a few people mentioned in the notes who furthered my understanding. To them and to all those unnamed but not forgotten, a thousand *terima kasihs*. The book may not do complete justice to all your work, but I hope it honors it in some way.

SUMATRA

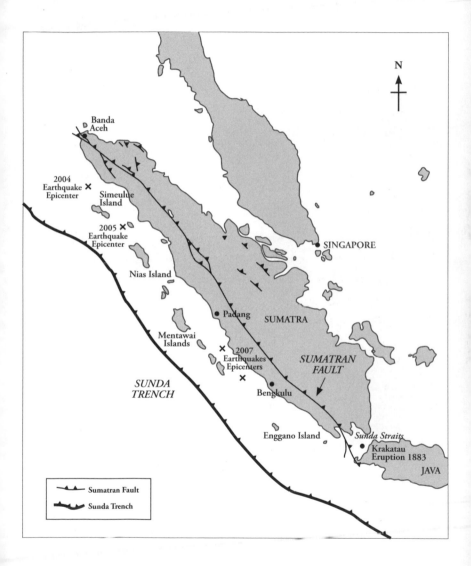

WESTERN SUMATRA

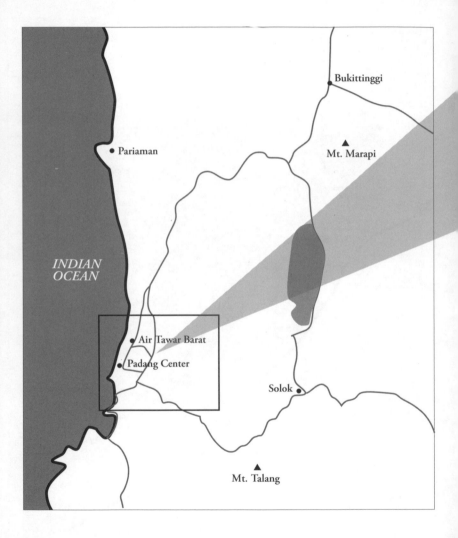

PADANG

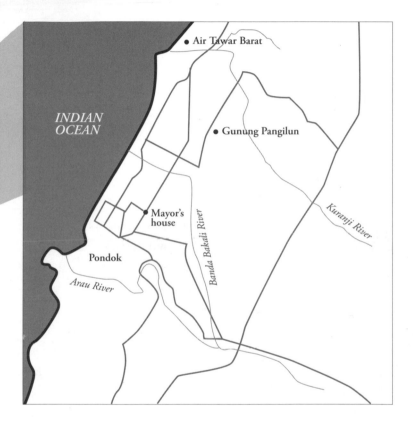

Introduction

Almost every time you go to a beach in Sumatra, you think, what if a tsunami came now? In mid-2007, not long after we've arrived in Banda Aceh, at Sumatra's northwest tip, I float on a surfboard off the beaches west of the city. A friend and I have lucked into a morning of meter-and-a-half walls of glassy, 25-degree water, peeling away to the right as they hit a dark reef, its mossy surface speckled with red and purple sponges clear as day down below. I'm a latecomer to the sport of surfing, so it's only taken me five or six chicken-hearted false starts to finally drop down the slick face of one of these waves. The rewards have been sweeter with each successive swell — effortless gliding in the power zone just under the wave's top lip.

Now my buddy has gone in and the wind is picking up. Time for one more. I look back toward the pithy, coral sand beach backed by steep limestone ridges draped in green, and sweep my gaze north past the low rock jetties of a shallow river mouth where a solitary man casts a fishing line into the surf. Behind him are some pinethistled casuarina trees known as *cemara* that managed to ride out the 2004 tsunami. The salt-tolerant trees used to grow so thick along the sand here that locals named this surf break after them. Now, there are only those few bedraggled sentinels left over there, along a rough-edged golf course. The tree trunks have been stripped of limbs and bark to at least 10 meters high. Scars from the last Big One, in 2004.

I start to build a picture of what sort of wall of water would need to come through *here*, where I'm floating, to get *there*, to the highest bare point on the trees, and the hair on the back of my neck stands up. The shoreline appears to recede. The water outside the breakers suddenly looks deep, endless, falling away into a black chasm that's conspiring out of sight. Would I even feel the earthquake? Would I have time to get in? Just when the day starts to bend into an alternate universe, I find that fisherman again. He hasn't moved. Presumably a survivor of the last tsunami, he looks as good a sensor as any. He's enough to beat back the welling shakes. I keep an eye on him, and line up one last wave.

The physical plant of Banda Aceh had healed so completely by the time we got there, that it took real imagination to recreate what had happened. Nearly US$8 billion in aid had seen to some of the best new infrastructure in Indonesia, in what had been one of its poorest places. There was enough money left over to help farmers and small business owners find new markets and new credit, programming that my wife, Hayley, worked on, and which was unheard of two and three years after other disasters around the world.

Acehnese had moved forward with a sense that the event, however dark, somehow fit into God's plans. A friend once asked me if one of my secular, free-will obsessed American cities back at home could ever have gotten over such a loss. The answer was not nearly as quickly. The same Islam we in the West always look upon warily had been an invaluable salve in Aceh. One of the popular views was that the Almighty was punishing Aceh for the separatist war against the young Indonesian state, a nasty 30-year conflict that had turned what was once the major launching point for the purifying Muslim *hajj* — the Veranda on Mecca — into a place where people couldn't trust their neighbors. The tsunami drove the two sides toward a peace deal in mid-2005. And so people were beginning to see a blessing in the disaster.

But every once in a while the ghosts would come out. One morning, several newly installed tsunami alarms went off by accident in coastal communities along the outskirts of the city. The crush of traffic trying to get through the city to safe ground made international news. But what I remember was the stone face of a housekeeper standing outside a friend's front door when I stopped by. Nothing I said could console her. Her eyes were dead set on the horizon to the west, on an ocean she couldn't see. And her mind was flashing back to a day she could see all too clearly.

Dislocation was a given even when people were standing on the restored ground they'd inhabited before the tsunami. It was a group of golfers who hammered home what a partial victory reconstruction would always be. They were former greens keepers and caddies at the city's only course, overlooking the surf breaks where the towering waves had come in among the *cemara* trees. In the aftermath, these men slowly built the course back with their own hands, clearing debris, then mowing crude greens to putt on, and fencing out the cattle. Nearly everyday they went out to play, circling the course as an act of moving forward and reclaiming a future from what the waves had taken. But it was also a daily act of remembrance for what they'd lost. "The place reminds me of my first wife," one of the greens keepers said while sitting near a mass grave at the edge of the old second tee one day. She'd supported him with money to develop his golf. If he skipped golf on his days off, she'd ask why he wasn't playing. She'd drowned in the tsunami, along with his infant child, while the guy was at the bank.

So when I heard about American scientist Kerry Sieh's hope to beat the next tsunami, which he was forecasting for another area of Sumatra's coast unaffected by the 2004 waves, I was drawn to the idea. Like everyone else, I wondered how the hell he could be so sure it was coming. And like everyone else in Aceh, witness or not, I thought that we should do everything in our power to avoid a repeat. When I met Kerry in the city of Padang, probable target of the next Big One; he bounced back and forth between optimism and pessimism. He thought people were too busy to think about something that might arrive ten years down the road, a predicament we lived that day when we ate lunch in a mall Sieh acknowledged was a death trap.

And yet he continued to encourage local friends who were educating folks in Padang. When I told him I wanted to shape a story about Padang and its struggles to understand what he was saying and what to do about it, he at first doubted anybody would care. But a few months later, he offered to take the project under the umbrella of the Earth Observatory of Singapore, a new research group he was starting: he, for one, did care. He understood that one of the ways we might avoid a repeat of Aceh, or any of the other deadly seismic events of the last decade, was to draw people into a story about a place trying to live with a looming threat. Here, it is

Padang. But it could just as easily be Manila or Kathmandu or Lima or even, in some respects, a wealthy place in Japan or the western United States that stares down an active fault line every day.

My hope is that the book joins a stream of popular conversation that flows around the Pacific Rim and beyond. Pass it on, and also let it push you out on a journey around your own place, to discover what lies underneath and to find stories of old events forgotten, imagine threads of resilience that need to take shape and acknowledge alternate futures, some of which we can work to avoid.

Oakley Brooks
Portland, Oregon

1.

Rocked

At midday on Monday the 10th of January 2005, Kerry Sieh, a geologist from California, settled in for a lunch of rice, curried fish and vegetables at a ramshackle, street-side café in the small port of a remote island off Sumatra, in Indonesia. He tuned into the flickering TV on the wall, and then held on for the ride of his life.

An Indonesian station had secured footage from a photographer who was setting up to film a wedding at the central Baiturrahman mosque in the city of Banda Aceh, at Sumatra's northwest tip, two weeks earlier, when the third largest earthquake ever recorded struck near the city. Soon after, the photographer turned his video camera out into the street toward a row of three-story brick and cement shophouses. The first shot of the film shows a couple of people pulling at a pile of bricks — the remnants of a collapsed building. After a few moments, clumps of people jog and walk swiftly down the street, chased by *labi-labi* minivans, some motorbikes, and a dump truck. Just faintly, in the way the people on foot are moving, you can see their confusion. Some are sprinting as if they have seen a monster. Others are walking dazed and not sure, it seems, which way is up. One man helps along a woman limping and holding her ribs. They are looking over their shoulder. There's a trickle of tar-colored water following them up the street, two-and-a-half kilometers from the ocean.

The water is quickly at people's heels. An older man walks out of his shop in the lower corner of the frame just as a knee-high surge arrives and he seems to lose his footing. Mercifully, the view of him obscures as crowds of frantic people hop up to the perch on top of the concrete outbuilding next to the cameraman. Out in the street, a minivan loses its grip on the pavement in the knee-deep flow, as the driver madly spins the steering wheel to fight it. It fishtails slowly in the current, then is flipped violently against the wall below and buried in a sudden river that's overwhelming the block. Just ten seconds after the leading edge, there's enough volume in the street that a massive hardwood tree — its green canopy taking up the entire width of the road — comes rushing past, before it too is turned under against the wall. Then a raft of ten cars washes by. The water is already one story deep. The wooden and aluminum remnants of entire neighborhoods follow in the water, flowing as if down a steep cataract. There are no bodies to see in this footage blurred by motion. But they are there, trapped under the debris. Survivors described the feeling of being deep inside a giant washing machine, with the contents of a lumberyard.

What is unnerving as the footage unfolds, and what one can hear in the pulsing screams of one woman watching behind the cameraman, is that there's no sign that the water will stop at one story — roughly the height of the wall they're on. In the midst of a city block, nobody can see where it's coming from. The water's mashed up so much of the city already, what's to say it won't consume the rest? But people have nowhere else to go. The grand yard of the mosque behind them has filled up with water as well. And nobody really even knows what they are looking at — a tsunami.

After a minute, an elderly guy in a black prayer cap suddenly emerges from the passenger side of a dark blue, floating SUV, and he's helped up onto the perch, beside the cameraman: his car drifted right to the videographer's feet.

The frame jumps to the ornate mosque, sometime later. The waters around it are calm and glassy but still floating cars. The photographer has survived. As the picture focuses, scores of people materialize on the roof of the mosque, just under its black-shingled, tear-shaped domes, and in the lower doorways and alcoves, hanging on to wrought iron screens and windows. A mass moves in a coconut tree nearby. It's a man clinging to the trunk up under the leaves, and he's adjusting his feet. How long has he been like that?

Kerry Sieh looked around the café at the handful of faces fixated on the tube, and he began to tear up. Would these folks, just out of range of the Aceh tsunami, be next?

The same tsunami-generating fault — shallow, powerful, and undersea — that created the Aceh disaster and led to more than 220,000 deaths that day around the Indian Ocean, also ran right under that restaurant he was sitting in. It started far away in eastern Indonesia, sliced west across the archipelago and then ripped north toward Myanmar. Sieh, then a spindly 54-year-old, had been studying the fault with Indonesian colleagues in these fringe islands for over a decade, and increasingly over the last few years, he felt that the section underneath was due for a dramatic jerk. He'd never ventured to Aceh, which had been mired in a nasty sectarian conflict. But the scientists could see these outer islands 1,000 kilometers south of Banda Aceh physically sinking, as the plates underneath ground into each other, building toward an explosive quake like the one 170 years ago.

Now, in these images from Aceh, he was seeing in real time what that break might mean. Angry, head-high waves of water could come ashore minutes after the earthquake, just as they had in Aceh. Not only were these islanders at risk, but on mainland Sumatra were two big cities facing these islands that held more than a million people combined. Other towns and fishing villages huddled all along the coast in between. By his count there were more vulnerable people around this section of fault than in Aceh, which had just lost 150,000 people in less than an hour.

All around him on the islands and on mainland Sumatra, as the videos looped on TV, word of new risks was also spreading from other scientists and talking heads on TV, through text messages that morphed conjectures into rumors and half truths and spread like the plague. Sieh and his colleagues had always struggled to explain this threat in the past. Now it had become too real, and people's imaginations were running wild.

As the scientists traveled through Sumatra's fringe islands by boat and helicopter to check instruments that track the islands' movement, they found awed residents in sandy, subsistence villages. These people, who had in past years looked askance at the strange researchers, were now following them around and hanging onto their every word. One islander suggested God had sent Sieh's group: how else had they known to put an instrument on the hill in his village that had apparently saved the town from Aceh's fate?

As Sieh's group flew in toward one hamlet near the equator, they found their hilltop global positioning instrument completely surrounded by tarp shelters and scores of villagers. The previous summer, the scientists had told them to go to high ground to avoid tsunami danger. Now locals were leaving nothing to chance with rumors flying about a closer, impending tsunami said to be arriving any day — they were staying high.

Later, on a neighboring island, scientists had to diffuse fears that they and their instruments helped *cause* the Aceh quake and powerful aftershocks felt from even hundreds of kilometers away. Several locals had cut the cord connecting the positioning unit to a satellite phone used to remotely download data, because they thought that U.S. President George W. Bush was remotely triggering the recent earthquakes through the equipment. Other rumors coursing through Sumatra had the United States setting off the earthquake and tsunami in Aceh with an atomic bomb or other explosion: why else would American military ships, under the cover of an aid mission, have been so quick to arrive in Aceh after the event?

A poster Sieh and colleagues had passed out the previous summer, showing how the islands moved up and down as a result of the active fault underneath, was also causing some concern. People believed the islands might sink forever — "like Atlantis," one of Sieh's collaborators says.

On mainland Sumatra, in the city of Padang which faced the islands, hoax text messages about an impending tsunami set off traffic jams on the routes to the city's highlands. People led their goats and cows up the hills. And even though many knew that there had been no earthquake to cause the waves, they went anyway. "I don't want to be considered arrogant," a girl cowering on an incline told a local reporter.

As Sieh and his crew moved further north, closer to the epicenter of the magnitude 9 quake in Aceh, the damage mounted — debris from wrecked houses, villages sitting in knee-deep water — and so did his frustration. He had to walk a fine line between trying to calm people down and asking them to be vigilant. He kept saying he wouldn't be there traveling around if he thought he was in danger. Yet he wanted them to think about where they might run in the event of a new tsunami and how much damage their low-lying villages might sustain. He thought it was almost certain they would see a big earthquake within 30 years, and the possibility looked real that tragedy might strike again before people were ready.

Sieh had already seen enough unheeded warnings. He'd walked through the despondent streets of Izmit, Turkey after a 1999 earthquake had leveled apartment buildings throughout the city and killed more than 17,000, in a place where geologists had been pointing up the risk for decades. Four years later, another known hotspot — the Iranian city of Bam — shook violently, taking the lives of at least 30,000 more. Already, reports were emerging of a Thai scientist who had pushed his government to brace for tsunamis on the recently leveled Andaman Coast as far back as 1998. He'd been hushed by tourist interests.

Sieh finally boiled over in front of a TV camera a few weeks after the Aceh devastation, channeling all the frustrations he and other geologists had built up watching these disasters happen.

"It's quite possible there will be a million person losses because of geological happenings in the 21st century," he said.

"You can't stand here and say a million people are going to

die," his Australian interviewer said incredulously, as they walked among tsunami debris.

"Sure." Sieh replied.

A moment later he added, "Well, I would love to have something done about it. But… a lot of us geologists feel like Jeremiah or John the Baptist, a voice calling in the wilderness. I know we are going to try our best to communicate what could happen and then we'll see what the leaders of the community, what the leaders of the country, want to do. But Indonesia isn't alone. Many, many countries have hazards like this and many countries will… given the status quo… lose hundreds of thousands of people."

2.
Evolution and Intuition

Sieh's words seem grimly prophetic now, half a decade later. Disasters have continued to hound us like lethal furies. After the tsunami came Hurricane Katrina, America's natural disaster debacle, which despite its relatively low death toll — around 1,800 — exposed deep vulnerabilities to natural hazards in the wealthiest country on earth. Just a month later, close to 86,000 people died in the mountainous region of Kashmir during a mid-range magnitude 7.6 earthquake.* Then, over the span of ten days in May 2008, nature packed a devastating one-two punch, first on the low-lying coast of insular Myanmar, where a cyclone drowned at least 130,000, then in Sichuan province of southwestern China, where a magnitude 7.9 earthquake toppled whole cities and schools and left at least 80,000 dead. Finally, 2010 started on a grisly note with a cynical magnitude 7.0 rumble for the failed state of Haiti: the final death toll of around 220,000 puts it among the seven worst earthquakes of all time.

---

* Magnitude here is *moment magnitude* which is what seismologists tend to use in measuring large earthquakes. Different from the Richter scale, moment magnitude is a factor of how much a fault slips during a quake and over how many kilometers the slipping action occurs.

Nobody near or far has been immune to these and other natural shockwaves, be it the poor and destitute on Port-au-Prince streets, the president who watched his palace twist and crunch, or the leaders of the free and not-so-free world.

Hurricane Katrina effectively ended George W. Bush's presidency, exposing a bullheaded incompetence that went right to the top of his administration and peeled off his remaining supporters. In China, the government was forced to go on an all-out offensive to silence parents, activists and journalists raising concerns and staging protest rallies about the faulty school construction — likened to 'tofu-dregs' — responsible for the death of more than 5,000 children. And in Taiwan, a botched response to a monsoon that left at least 400 dead in 2009 led to the resignation of the country's prime minister. After Myanmar's military junta — afraid to open the country and to be seen as weak — limited entry by the United Nations and other aid groups for days after Cyclone Nargis, UN Secretary General Ban Ki-moon himself stepped up to negotiate an opening to aid.

Damages in 2008 totaled $200 billion across the world, or about the GDP of Israel. In stable financial centers like Munich, Geneva and Singapore, re-insurance executives, whose companies sell insurance for insurers all over the world, were gaping at the damage losses they would have to cover: $45 billion in 2008. But the industry had paid that total after just one event — Katrina is their highest single-instance loss ever. All told, a hurricane-ravaged 2005 cost insurers $90 billion.

But the money pales compared to the cumulative human toll. Over the last decade, more than a million people have died in natural disasters.

And the consensus is that serious threats loom. Sieh was far from being the only geologist talking about a single million-man disaster and scientists' greatest area of concern usually centers on the area along the southern edge of Asia. Here, in an arc that stretches through mainly developing countries from Turkey in the east to the Philippines in the west, overcrowded cities sit over the top of a massive geological shifting zone — the point where various plates collide with the giant one under Eurasia. Massive earthquakes have rocked places like Istanbul, Tehran, Karachi, Delhi, Dhaka, Kathmandu, Manila and Jakarta in centuries past. But in the struggle to industrialize, to consolidate wobbly, hungry nations facing massive urban migrations, few cities are informed by their earthquake history. Tehran, the site of destructive earthquakes four times in the last 1,200 years, is now a shoddily built mega city on an active fault with a daytime population as high as 12 million. Many of the poor commuters sleep in mud-brick structures, which are cool at night but tend to collapse and crush their inhabitants in a quake. This is ground zero for experts' disaster fears. But rapid urbanization everywhere puts all sorts of people at risk. We're now more of an urban species than a rural one for the first time in history, and by some estimates more than 470 million people in rich countries and poor ones now live in cities within 200 kilometers of active faults capable of large earthquakes.

Climate change will only pile on more misery. Insurers are already blaming rising damage tolls from hurricanes and cyclones on global warming. The more pronounced threats of sea-level rise and extreme drought wait. Sea levels are rising faster than projections at the turn of the century said they would. Many scientists are already predicting at least a meter of rise by 2100 and that's without knowing what will happen to the massive West Antarctic or Greenland ice sheets. One can start to see why the United Nations estimates 200 million migrants due to environmental causes by 2050, a virtual new class of people.

Everybody agrees that the suffering must end (except maybe TV news executives). The UN spent a decade focusing on disaster reduction in the 1990s. We know that money spent to help people and places anticipate and guard against disaster is a better investment than picking up the pieces afterward. We're at this technological, hyperconnected zenith, with a burgeoning understanding of seismic and weather risks. Yet tens of thousands of people are still sitting ducks in a storm. Certainly, buildings are safer in wealthy countries that abide by modern construction codes, which allowed a place like Chile to avoid high death tolls during a magnitude 8.8 earthquake in early 2010. And there are rays of hope in poorer countries too. In coastal Bangladesh, repeatedly battered by devastating cyclones, word of an approaching storm now spreads from the national meteorological agency to a network of volunteers, who circle dense neighborhoods on bicycles and foot and shout through handheld megaphones, urging people to seek shelter in new elevated concrete platforms. From losing 138,000 people in a 1991 cyclone, the toll dropped to under 4,000 in a similar one that hit in 2007.

But for every step forward, in places that had fresh memories of loss, there were other places that bumbled in the face of threats even when people had the time and the information to get out of the way. In New Orleans, evacuation orders went out well before Hurricane Katrina hit, but people chose to ignore them or didn't understand what they meant and remained below sea level in some of the city's most vulnerable neighborhoods. Myanmese were warned over national TV about the approaching Cyclone Nargis, but generally didn't understand the severity of the situation and stayed in the Irrawaddy River delta as the storm raked it with tide-like surges up to four meters deep.

These people showed clearly that we can surround hazardous places with the best prediction and interpretation technology in the world, but unless people on the ground invest in knowing the threat, the technology fizzles out in their inaction. Beating earthquakes depends on strong laws that govern how buildings are constructed, but the reality is that in developing countries, where money is tight and governance thin, the strength of a home or office is really up to the owner. Istanbul has updated its building codes but recent apartment blocks in the swelling city appear so quickly, they are said to have 'landed overnight', with little oversight and many cheap materials. Volcanoes will usually give off enough warning for evacuations before they send hot, dangerous mudflows down their flanks. But moving out of the way still often depends on individuals and there have been high-profile cases of communities refusing evacuation orders, not least along the slopes on Mount Merapi in Java, in 2006. Across the Pacific outside Los Angeles, people still insist on living in hillside homes repeatedly assaulted by quick-developing debris flows driven by heavy rains.

The next Sumatran tsunami poses a dilemma, with human decision in mind. Some education could, theoretically, help people avoid death in low-lying areas along the coast. When a big quake rattles the walls* for an extended period of time, it's a strong signal to get to higher ground. But a tsunami only gives you a small window of time to react, before it arrives. Sumatra might not have more than

---

It usually starts with an undersea earthquake, but rare landslides and volcanoes can also be the culprits — the most famous being the 1883 eruption of Krakatau, which collapsed the volcanic cone of an island into the strait between Sumatra and Java and sent out tsunami waves as high as 42 meters.

a few minutes, being so close to the fault line. And this led to a debate after the 2004 tsunami.

Many in the diplomatic and scientific community pushed for a new high-tech warning program that could spur quick evacuations in Indonesia, as part of a new system for the entire Indian Ocean. Donations and expertise poured in from Japan, Russia, China, America and Germany, the latter pledging 45 million Euros towards Indonesia's system. The Indonesian president charged its builders to get a warning out to tsunami-prone areas within five minutes of a major earthquake. Local scientists and technophiles on the vulnerable Sumatran coast looked forward to the system. "Look, after an earthquake, you're totally numb," a veteran of Sumatran earthquakes and a warning system advocate said. "It's bullshit if you can talk and think in that period."

But a vocal minority, including Sieh, doubted that people on the ground could actually get an accurate warning from a monitoring system in time. The detractors argued the money would be better spent on educating people to move to high ground immediately after they felt heavy, prolonged shaking — likely from the undersea fault. Properly taught, people could evacuate on their own judgement.

A high stakes test emerged. The warning system would take several years to develop and even when it was up and running, it wouldn't cover the islands closest to the earthquake zone — the ones where Sieh's group worked. Education might have an opportunity to prove its worth. But efforts would have to build up people's response to be almost instinctive, so they wouldn't think in that lull before a tsunami, so much as react.

***

On December 26, 2004, the earthquake shaking originated with fault movement off Aceh and spread north at least 1,300 kilometers into the Andaman Sea east of India. In a beachside national park in Sri Lanka, where the shaking was light but the sea nonetheless receded, three elephants turned from the coast, shrieked and ran to higher ground. In coastal Thailand, where shaking was also light but the ocean backed out, elephants used for tourist rides bucked handler instructions and ran away. A herd of water buffalo in another Thai coastal village turned tail and ran to the top of a nearby hill. People in Sri Lanka and Sumatra also told of flocks of flamingoes, bats and egrets flying away from the coast ahead of the tsunami's arrival.

What triggered them has been confounding observers and scientists since the Greek historian Diodorus wrote that rats, snakes and centipedes left the city of Helice in 373 BC before a major earthquake hit. Centuries later, authorities went so far as to evacuate apartment blocks in the Chinese city of Haicheng in the winter of 1974–75, when snakes began leaving their underground lairs in droves — considered a sign of an impending quake. A magnitude 7 quake did strike there in early February of 1975, and people who'd fled the city or moved to small makeshift huts survived.

But later reports suggested the snakes might have been abandoning hibernation because it was unseasonably warm. And despite huge investments and decades-long experiments trying to pinpoint any earthquake precursors that animals might be reacting to — strange gases or changes in humidity or low frequency rumblings that humans can't detect — scientists have so far been unable to nail down any consistent markers that tip off earthquakes.

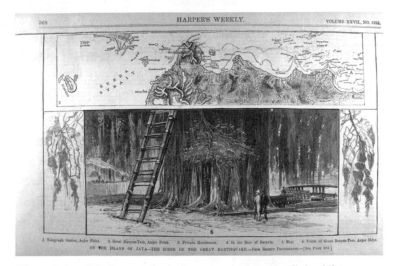

The explosion of Krakatau unleashed a tsunami 13 stories tall that left its mark in South Sumatra. (Courtesy of Earthquake Engineering Laboratory, UC Berkeley)

But one geobiologist in California has suggested that animals native to tsunami-prone areas could have easily evolved, over millions of years, an instinctive sense of tsunamis. The signs are no mystery — the earthquake comes, the tide line shifts wildly and the water eventually recedes, then the waves come back in toward shore, often with a loud rumble that humans can hear, minutes before the waves actually appear. The trick is hard-wiring into an animal's genes the relationship between the signs and the instincts to run, so an animal will do it even if it's never experienced the destructive force of a tsunami. Animals have shown that learned behaviors can be inherited from generation to generation. Bees, for instance, communicate the location of nectar to fellow hive mates through a dance, once they return from a particularly good site. This behavior has been proven to be instinctive, not learned. Scientists say it must have evolved from experimental communication that was eventually encoded in genes and passed down. Assuming that some animals drown in each tsunami event, nature would slowly select those who run away after an earthquake triggers the progression of tsunami signs and then the waves. Over the course of 500 million years, that behavior becomes ingrained into the surviving groups — a part of its genes — and a tsunami-resilient population develops along the coast.

"The problem of a tsunami escape response in animals is much easier to believe than a warning response for an earthquake near the epicenter," Prof. Joseph Kirschvink told a reporter after the 2004 tsunami. "A tsunami happens after a big quake, and there are obvious signals that one is approaching."

Humans have been able to refine traits that help with survival, and we've even been able to do it in a relatively short amount of time. Tibetans have inherited ways for their blood to cope with low oxygen levels in their elevated homeland, and the genes that control that trait are thought to have become common as recently as 3,000 years ago. We've even shown that recent changes in habits can affect our genes: adults can now digest milk because we have a greater presence of the lactose-tolerant gene than our ancestors — presumably because drinking milk into adulthood has become advantageous and widely practiced. But the trouble with developing innate tsunami reactions is most of us haven't stayed in one place long enough to hone the trait, especially when the feedback driving the behavior — a destructive tsunami — comes so rarely.

More importantly, in the modern world our very biology resists learning and adapting to these threats, because we're so focused on how we do in the economy of today, not how our relatives do generations from now. In some cases, more successful short-term survival builds in a sort of long-term amnesia and vulnerability. Maybe relatives living in an earthquake and tsunami-prone area pass down a house or a business in a prime locale along the main harbor. But that house eventually comes tumbling down because it's been built on marshland, which amplifies the shaking. And that prime location on the waterfront becomes a death trap when the tsunami funnels up through the harbor. Kerry Sieh calls this the "tyranny of the urgent".

"We just haven't evolved to the point where we can deal with these intermittent events," Sieh says. "Take the example of people in Aceh, about 600 years ago. We think a tsunami came then and maybe wiped out half the population. The other half? They go ahead and rebuild right in the same place. There's nothing in their gene pool that causes people to rebuild in order to avoid long-term destruction, to prevent that happening to their grandchildren. You just can't expect people to have an inbred desire to respond to an event that occurs once every 600 years or every 200 years."

The way to overcome our dulled senses and the corners we've painted ourselves into is by building a new layer of culture on top of the one we already have. This isn't easy, because so much of how we live is built to resist these new practices.

The Japanese have been working on it for millennia.

Coastal Japan, mirrored by offshore faults, is the most tsunami-prone place on earth. About 35 events deliver waves over one meter in height every century. People have been passing down stories of tsunamis past and learning to think in that calm between earthquakes and tsunamis nearly as long as they've been thinking at all. Written accounts of devastating, fatal floods go back to AD 684.

The word *tsunami* — which combines the Japanese characters for 'harbor' and 'waves' — first appears in shogunate records describing the 1611 waves that killed thousands of people in northeast Honshu Island. Spanish explorer Sebastian Vizcaino described people scurrying for the hills in an inlet in that region just as the tsunami was hitting; whether in anticipation of the waves or upon seeing them approaching it's not certain.

But in 1700, when a tsunami sent from a North American earthquake arrived on that same coast, people fled ahead of it, some clearly at the behest of what must have been a sharp village head. He wouldn't have felt the major earthquake centered off the coast of what are today the U.S. states of Oregon and Washington; he would only have had the strange tide-like surges to tip him off before the waves arrived.

A similarly vigilant chief in southwestern Honshu kept some of his flock out of an 1854 tsunami and became a legend for it. Hamaguchi Goryo, a benevolent soy sauce manufacturer, was apparently near his hillside rice fields and looking out at the seashore after an earthquake, when he saw the water recede. He'd heard stories of past tsunamis and recognized the signs. So he set all of his stacks of rice on fire to attract the attention of villagers below. As many as nine people ran up toward the fire — moths to light — and were saved. Others in town drowned.

The story of survival took on new weight, however, after an 1896 tsunami approached 40 meters tall in some places on Honshu's northern coast and left almost 22,000 people dead. The next year, Hamaguchi appeared as a character in a new tale called 'The Living God', by a Japanese speaking Irish-Greek expatriate writer named Lafcadio Hearn (Hearn, who later gained Japanese citizenship,

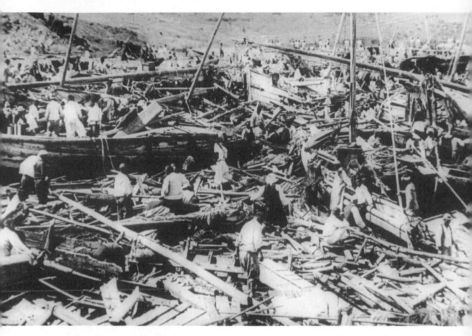

An earthquake in 1933 off the Japanese city of Kamaishi, in northern Honshu, sent a tsunami into the city's harbor. (Courtesy of Earthquake Engineering Laboratory, UC Berkeley)

introduced *tsunami* into the English dictionary). Hearn's dramatic story delivers great returns for the chief's identification of the signs of a tsunami, his presence of mind to do something about it, and his willingness to sacrifice his rice harvest for the good of the village: he secures the safety of the entire fictional village, not simply the nine that survived in reality. And the mores, as well as the safety lesson, lent the story staying power. It appeared in school readers across the country following a 1933 tsunami. It later reached school children in a book published in the northwest United States and even spread across the world in an animated cartoon.

Hamaguchi's legacy and his legend have become intertwined

with the physical plant in his old village. He funded the construction of a five-meter dirt sea wall to cut down the energy of future tsunami waves. Today, he's depicted on the wall's updated cement facade, bearing a brightly burning torch and leading the villagers to safety, and the village's current residents commemorate the event with an annual ceremony and work party to spruce up stands of sumac trees around the wall.

Other towns in coastal Japan maintain protective greenbelts backed by seawalls built by their ancestors. In northeast Honshu, people mark the anniversaries of past events with a walk to monuments that mark the outer edge of the tsunamis' flood. They can see clearly the names of victims past, etched into the walls of Shinto shrines up and down the coast. All the stark reminders and the stories are built into the latest tsunami motto in northeast Honshu: *Save yourself.*

In recent decades, however, as the Japanese have added high technology to their arsenal, officials have noticed that self-responsibility in the event of a tsunami has lagged. A national network of seismic and wave sensors can send out tsunami warnings through local sirens and broadcasters in a matter of minutes, but many citizens stay at home and watch the TV waiting for instructions, instead of heading for high ground immediately after an earthquake. Others loll in false security behind newly built walls and a network of tsunami gates that are supposed to keep tsunami surges out of rivers and harbors. It turns out that walls will only diminish, not entirely stop deadly tsunamis. And river gates cannot always be closed in time to stop a surge. Even after all these centuries, people still react to strong earthquake shaking and warning alarms by traveling toward the sea to check out the potential tsunami waves, which could prove deadly given how close Japan is to tsunami-triggering faults and how quickly the waves arrive. Local governments on Honshu have lately redoubled efforts to educate school kids on the finer points of tsunami behavior.

What complicates attempts to educate and protect people there, as well as around the world, is that in those 15 minutes between earthquake and tsunami, even the well-informed skew the threat with all sorts of personal inhibitions and limitations. In one city, people may all learn the same lessons of how to run from impending doom. But our disaster experience is affected by things like how rich we are, how we view the world, and how tight our surrounding community is. At a surface level, this makes intuitive sense. An agnostic may not think about or prepare for hurricane threats in the same way as a fundamentalist Christian or devout Hindu. A wealthy homeowner with a fire resistant roof and a friend in the city fire department is better positioned as a wildfire approaches than the migrant worker in a nearby canyon who can't speak the local language and who's ended in the path of the fireball because he has nowhere else to live.

Broader events leading up to the disaster, like wars and depressions, bear on how people respond. Japanese villagers talked about but never built protective walls and new curriculums in schools after an 1896 disaster, because money was tight for education and other necessities in the aftermath of the war against China over Manchuria; they suffered for little preparation in a whopping 1933 tsunami. Similarly, Acehnese on the Sumatran mainland had, in fact, suffered a deadly tsunami as recently as 1964, but as one Indonesian tsunami scientist notes, "We were too busy fighting each other to pay attention to these things." Aceh separatists took up arms against the new Indonesian state run from Jakarta beginning in the mid-1970s (and only finally made peace as a result of the 2004 tsunami). During the war, the province became one of the poorest places in Indonesia, especially in the rural villages where both sides routinely burned schools and government buildings and exacted protection payments. Acehnese villagers said after the tsunami that they had been fearful of escaping to the mountains, where combatants hid out.

But in tracking how micro groups fare in disaster, the poor don't always fare poorly. And this makes a powerful case for the importance of knowledge as a weapon. It turns out that the strongest demonstrated sense for tsunamis recently has not been in relatively wealthy, well-schooled and technologically advanced Japan but on one isolated island off the coast of Aceh, right next the epicenter of the 2004 quake.

Like Japanese areas, this island, called Simeulue (pronounced 'simaloo') suffered a devastating tsunami in its past. When a violent quake shook just before midday on Friday, January 4 in 1907, unassuming men — or maybe humbled ones — followed up the earthquake with their usual Friday prayers. But any seaside mosques on the island's west coast turned into watery graves. At one house of prayer, a ten-meter wall of water tore through the building and the waves knocked out historical stone pillars said to have come from the sultan in Banda Aceh. The surge left the dead up in the branches of trees, alongside bloated buffalo (presumably non-natives without escape instincts). It lifted dolphins and sharks into flooded rice paddies. One story holds that ripping currents supposedly carried a woman 20 kilometers south along the coast, around several headlands, to another village where she married and raised a family. Another survivor bided his time in the top of a breadfruit tree, chomping on its fruits, until the water receded that evening. People were also said to take refuge near the beachside tomb of the first Islamic teacher on the island, and survived the waves without a scratch. These mind-bending yarns, no doubt spiced up, traveled across the years, along with the simple grave of a man who supposedly drowned while leaving the mosque in one village, the faint '1907' etched on his wizened, rectangular tomb left alongside the restored building.

In the local tongue, a single word — *smong* — came to describe the whole phenomenon now known worldwide as the typical tsunami sequence — an earthquake, followed by the water receding quickly from streams, rivers and the ocean shallows, and then a series of waves that drove deep into the landscape. People learned the meaning of *smong* from their grandparents in the evenings or in the fields in casual stories. Sometimes the elders were prompted as they happened upon corals that had been lifted by the tsunami and deposited in rice paddies and hillside fruit and nut gardens. Because nearly every family was affected, the stories were almost always personal. The tales often ended with an admonishment to run to high ground if the process of *smong* started. Parents also conjured the idea of *smong* when they were angry and threatening their children, as in "I'm going to swallow you like a *smong*!".

But what made Simeulue's oral history so powerful was also the place where it survived.

The island grew slowly in the three generations since 1907, staying mostly rural and oriented around villages and their low, square mosques and remaining dominated by ethnic Simeulueans who assimilated a trickle of outsiders.

The dagger-shaped island is also punctuated with a ridge of ascendable hills that consistently give coastal dwellers an escape platform. In 2002, Simeulueans got a practice run for the real thing when a magnitude 7.3 earthquake struck on a small patch of fault that runs through the middle of the island. No tsunami came, but villagers briefly fled to the hills and some even reported establishing temporary camps there. Elders who knew the 1907 story well took the time to explain why they were *not* running: the creek estuaries had not drained out.

By the time the 2004 tsunami came, people knew where to go and when to go there. Waves rolled in 9 meters high, starting just 10 minutes after the earthquake. And they stripped coastal mosques to their pillars again. This time nobody was near them. Of the more than 78,000 people on the island, seven died in the tsunami. One was a man who knew the old story well but tried to beat the tsunami by rushing back toward his house on his motorbike between the first and second waves, to get some family documents. When researchers interviewed villagers after the event, three-quarters of them had heard of the stories of the 1907 tsunami.

3.
From Amnesia to Activism

Eight hundred kilometers from the epicenter of the Aceh quake, in the West Sumatran city of Padang, Patra Rina Dewi, a 31-year-old non-profit worker, felt a long, harmless swaying. Then she saw clips of the flood sweeping through Banda Aceh; "the water was so dark and fast. Nobody could swim in it." And she had no idea the two events were related. Patra was a scientist herself, trained in Malaysia in plant tissue culture, the practice of growing new plant buds in the laboratory from the stems of a parent plant. She'd grown up in a household of educators — her mother lectured in biology at the local Andalas University and her father was a middle-school teacher who later worked for the local department of education. Around the New Year, 2005, Patra was at home with her family, in their tranquil seaside neighborhood in Padang, considering a request from her advisor in Malaysia to return for a PhD.

But she'd never heard of a tsunami.

She thought the earthquake and tsunami were two entirely

separate events. As more and more scientists appeared on TV linking the two, the video began to make sense. The quake had caused this rapid ocean flood. "That was just my first lesson in tsunamis," she says.

A few days later, Patra's younger sister Ulya, a doctor, traveled to the disaster zone in Aceh with a mercy mission out of Padang organized by two American surf journalists. Their destination was the island of Simeulue. For nine days, the relief group worked the coastal villages from an 80-foot motor-sailboat normally used for chartered surfing trips, handing out food and giving first aid to shivering, shocked people sick from exposure in the wet climate. Ulya noticed that in hillside camps, people were cooking with utensils they'd grabbed before they ran away from the tsunami. And slowly it became clear to her and to others doing relief around the island, that nearly all Simeulueans had survived.

When the aid group returned to Padang, Patra strong-armed her way to a meeting with the relief organizers, "I told Ulya she had to introduce me to them." Patra has big brown eyes, and full lips that break into an infectious smile. She seems to radiate more charm when her round face is encircled with one of her rainbow of headscarves and she wields an academic English, honed through special tutoring she got in the evenings as a kid. She earned a spot on the next boat mission to Simeulue as a 'field nurse'.

At a trying time and in a desolate landscape — houses leveled to their foundations and villages stripped of every last twig of vegetation — her relief crew found a glimmer of light in people gleefully telling their survival secret in Simeulue. There was a way to beat this monster. "Every villager in the islands told us: when the ocean goes out it will come back angry. They knew to go to higher ground," says Matt George, one of the relief organizers. "Here we are 20 miles from the epicenter and the drowned bodies we found cruising in the channel weren't island people. They were dressed like city folk, with formal clothes and hard shoes," likely drifted out from the Aceh mainland.

After a third trip on the relief boat in mid-February, George went to the U.S. to round up more relief funding. He returned in March bearing the latest copy of *National Geographic*, with a tsunami-related story inside entitled 'Where Next?'. In the accompanying map showing the world's densest cities near undersea fault lines, Padang, population 800,000, stuck out like a sore thumb, at a density of 141,000 people-per-square-coastal-kilometer. The jagged line of the Sumatran megathrust loomed offshore. Patra was caught off guard when she saw the graphic. She and her volunteer colleagues had somehow missed the media chatter about the risk on the fault offshore of Padang, her home city.

Now when the streets jammed up with fleeing people, cars and motorbikes after a series of smaller but closer quakes in March and April, it looked like more than a nuisance. People were in jeopardy, stuck and helpless if a tsunami came. Everybody was discovering that they lived in a city built as if the phenomenon of tsunamis didn't exist.

***

The Minangkabau, the dominant ethnic group of West Sumatra, were not beach dwellers until quite recently. Their heartland, to which Patra Dewi's family traces its roots, is in the hill country to the east. Their civilization is said to have evolved from a relative of Alexander the Great who landed in a great flood on the top of Mount Marapi, the most prominent volcano of the Minang highlands. People spread out across the rich volcanic soil around Marapi, forming clans that traced their bloodlines through their mothers and cultivated rice in the cool, mosquito-free uplands. Lucrative gold mines and later a brisk trade in coffee, pepper and other spices made the high country attractive. As Europeans and other foreign interests increasingly dominated the Sumatran coast, the highlands — which had always offered security — also insulated the Minang from the constant pressure of outside cultural influence. In one of the defining myths of the Minang heritage, the locals try to fend off an encroaching army from Java. Just before a large battle, the Minang suggest a fight between both camps' best buffaloes in lieu of bloodshed. The Javanese agree and send a muscle-bound hulk of an animal. The Minang send a calf, with a blade strapped to its head. Meeting in the middle, the calf beguiles the bull by going to suckle at his belly. But as the calf butts him to start the flow of milk, he gores him to death with the unseen dagger. The Javanese, at least in this instance, are beaten back. The cunning Minangkabau (which means 'victorious buffalo' in the local tongue) score a victory for soft power, for female-centric matrilineal customs, for mountainous peculiarity.

Southeast Asian historian Anthony Reid, who's spent more than 40 years studying Sumatra, believes that repeated tsunamis might have even made the coast less hospitable and seemingly dangerous through the centuries. Virtually no attention was paid to this phenomenon before the Aceh quake and tsunami. ("I've written untold books about Sumatra and never once mentioned earthquakes," Reid lamented afterward.) But after watching the tsunami scour Aceh, analysts are looking with new eyes at the frequency of events in the historical record and sensing that the shifting rivers, flooded coastal plains and general fear surrounding ocean intrusion might be a reason that the Minang and many ethnic groups up and down Sumatra favored the highlands over the west coast.

In West Sumatra, the population patterns are striking. More than 90% of the population of the area lived in the highlands during the period of the last big tsunamis, around 1800. It wasn't until 1990, after 45 years of Indonesia's post-independence growth, that coastal areas in the province had as many people as the settlements in the hills.

Padang's port, originally put on the map by the colonizing Dutch in the late 1600s, continued as a conduit for the region's

An artist's engraving of a Sumatran tsunami following the 1861 earthquake in northern Sumatra. (Courtesy of Earthquake Engineering Laboratory, UC Berkeley)

traditional natural resources and newer ones like palm, coal and cement mixed with local lime. The city grew into the hub of government and finance for the province and dozens of government ministries sprung up along the main north-south thoroughfare originally laid by the Dutch from the harbor to the highlands; the buildings' Soviet-looking facades rise into buffalo horn-themed vaulting rooflines. The place also became the education center for all of central Sumatra, eventually drawing more than 36,000 students.

Two of them were Patra Dewi's parents, who arrived for university in 1965. In the mid-1970s, the prestigious Andalas University and the state university of Padang bought parcels of a coconut plantation along the beach north of the city center, at the mouth of the Kuranji River, and they opened it up for professors and lecturers to live on. The place was a former battlefield and considered a swampy wasteland that was full of snakes. But Patra's parents became one of the first five families to move there in 1977. They tracked a rudimentary road out to their sandy plot, which sits on a barrier island separated from the mainland by a narrow canal. Contractors built them a two-story cement house, with a third-story attic and a wide, covered breezeway out front. Over the years, the yard has grown into a happy riot filled with chickens and ducks and two ponds full of fish. All around them, the neighborhood has filled in along a network of gridded dirt roads, with academics' simple tin-roofed houses and rows of one-story rooming tracts for students.

In this quiet period for tsunamis, the rest of Padang's growth also clung to the coastal strip — that narrow padang or 'field' between sea and mountains that had originally given the place its name. From the top of Gunung Pangilun, a solitary hump of a hill just a kilometer from Patra's house, you get a sense of how wedged in the city is, in its warrens of brick and concrete and corrugated metal roofs perched next to a silvery sea. The buses growl and motorbikes moan along the few arteries, throwing up a light haze. Behind the hill, rice paddies and coconut palms give way quickly to the steep, undeveloped and untracked mountains of the Bukit Barisan range, which runs along Sumatra's spine.

It's the most scenic city in Sumatra, but a worse one for tsunami danger couldn't have been imagined.

The thing is, a city is living and breathing. It's more than bricks and mortar. It has a collective psyche, and that can change. Padang was, after the Aceh tsunami, looking dicey to people like Patra not only because it sat there facing the fault but also because it was stuck in an ignorant smog. It had no culture for responding. There were no well-known artifacts to draw upon — flood markers, displaced corals, deeply felt stories. (Rural elders told an old myth about the earth sitting in the horns of a buffalo who shook his head to cause an earthquake, but Patra deemed it 'stupid' and of little value in the city.)

Patra and other local and American volunteers began piecing together what they could find to start building that culture. The Aceh footage had been a wake up call. The lessons from the island of Simeulue showed people could learn where to run and when to run before a tsunami hit. And the volunteer group in Padang also began reaching out to scientists.

In late April of 2005, Matt George and some of the other American volunteers met Kerry Sieh at the Batang Arau hotel, a hangout on the Arau River for foreign surfers headed to the outer islands off Sumatra. Later, they brought Patra and Ulya to meet Sieh and Danny Natawidjaja and began to learn the basics behind the tsunami threat. The group wanted to know if Padang's beach communities would have enough time after an earthquake to reach a high point, before the waves struck. Sieh said they would have 15 to 30 minutes.

In May and June, the tsunami activists began teaching people close to the beach how to make their escape. One of the new engines for the group was an Andalas engineering professor, Febrin Ismail, who rallied university students to pass out information flyers about the threat and announce plans for their first evacuation drill in the neighborhoods around Gunung Pangilun. Febrin and his group worked the neighborhood with a homemade sign strung between bamboo poles. Fueled by local school kids, that first Saturday evacuation to the hill drew 3,000 people from the surrounding communities. A month later, several hundred people anchored by university students mustered for another march all the way from the beach toward Gunung Pangilun. The mayor of Padang, Fauzi Bahar, arrived for the walk in a tracksuit and reluctantly accepted a commendation plaque that some of George's compadres had arranged from the city of San Francisco ("I haven't done anything yet," Fauzi told the group). He took some pictures and then climbed in a car adorned with loudspeakers and led the group off on its journey with rap music blaring, before peeling out of sight.

Many people all over town shared the mayor's ambivalence about this new tsunami activism. They seemed willing to join or help as long as it didn't disturb the normal course of their day. The city's information minister loaned canvassers a loudspeaker truck in exchange for approving their handouts, but when organizers tried to draw in the city's social affairs minister for funding, he didn't offer any help: he was worried about people's fragile mental state. After all, these were the same jumpy citizens that were running away at the mere mention of a tsunami on hoax text messages. While the fire chief participated in drills, the city's tourism chief told Patra she and her colleagues were chasing tourists away with all their talk. In early 2005, the Aceh tsunami had been bad for business in West Sumatra, with the industry claiming a $23 million loss as visitors were passing up Padang and even the popular hill station of Bukittinggi, in the heart of traditional Minangkabau homes and markets. The tsunami canvassers were now a convenient scapegoat.

In the neighborhoods, the volunteers encountered a lot of resistance from people who didn't want to leave their homes for drills because they worried about burglars. Patra remembers people asking the canvassers facetiously if they wanted to invite the tsunami, as if by talking about the phenomenon it became more real. In a way, it did: that was the point. But it's not a reality anybody really wants to embrace.

So keeping things quiet and downplaying the risk looked like a good option for local leaders. But it was a hard stance to maintain. In one memorable turn of events, the mayor went from distractedly text-messaging his way through a meeting with George, Patra, and some other volunteers about an evacuation drill, to asking them breathlessly for help a few days later. A quake had just given the city a strong but harmless jolt and caused a nearby volcano to smoke. Could her group assemble an evacuation scheme for the whole city? the mayor asked. President Susilo Bambang Yudhoyono was showing up the next day for a tour of West Sumatra to calm jittery nerves, and he wanted to know what Padang was doing to prepare for a tsunami. The next day, Matt George stood by a hastily drawn flow chart at the city's newly anointed disaster headquarters — a former tourism office by the beach — and the president said to him, with the news cameras rolling, "Thank you for your hard work… It helps a lot to innocent people."

It was on those slivers of support that the new movement built. In a house loaned by a local road builder and with funds from Bambang Winarto, a prominent spice merchant, they started their own locally based group, Komunitas Siaga Tsunami ('Tsunami Alert Community'), shortened to Kogami. Not surprisingly, Winarto was unwilling to give up his lucrative business, which processed West Sumatra's sweet cinnamon bark, shipped most of it to the United States and was dependent on the port of Padang like generations of traders before him. But he saw that continuing on in the city required guarding against it all being taken away — a modern place packed with people and leveled like Aceh. So he and the other Kogami backers enabled Patra and two other recent graduates to lead a pack of a hundred volunteers fanning out in black T-shirts across the city to spread the word about tsunamis, and the leadership also returned to scientists like Sieh. The organizers hoped to get a sharper sense of the risk, a sense Sieh and his colleagues had been honing over the last decade and a half.

4.
Hidden in Plain Sight

Kerry Sieh did not come to Sumatra to save it. He came in search of professional glory. He wanted to say something definitive about big dangerous faults and California's infamous San Andreas Fault wasn't cooperating. As a student and a professor in California, he pioneered the physical study of historical earthquakes. His proving ground beginning in the mid-1970s was the old lake and riverbeds along the San Andreas, which slices diagonally across the middle of California. At Pallett Creek, a site just outside Los Angeles, he detailed 1,500 years of past major earthquakes left in peat and sands disturbed by the fault. He showed convincingly that the San Andreas tended to rupture in a major event at that site about once every 130 years.

By the late 1980s it had been longer than 130 years since the last big crack, but Sieh couldn't say for certain if the next Big One was coming soon. Sometimes the San Andreas rested 300 years between majors; sometimes it erupted in only 45. What caused the irregularity was a mystery, and solving that mystery in California was beginning to look impossible. It would take a decade or more to develop another research site like Pallett Creek, and the dating technique he and his team were using — measuring the amount of carbon decayed in the earth's organic matter — usually left a margin of error of 50 years. Sieh, who has a boyish, sun-kissed native Californian face also has an impatience about him, a desire to overachieve — in a lot of ways he's the opposite cast of a prototypical geologist, picking over rocks while his beard grays. Even though he was just 40 at the close of the 1980s, he cringed thinking of himself turning into his own layer of sediment before contributing something meaningful to the science of large faults. "I wasn't going to get enough precise data in my lifetime or the lifetime of my students even," he says. He needed a new fault.

In 1991, an American colleague sent Sieh to Indonesia to help describe the movement of a major, San Andreas-like fault that runs down the middle of Sumatra. Sumatra is one of those dynamic, chaotic meeting points of geological plates along the Pacific Rim. Here, the top crust of Southeast Asia collides with that of Australia and that underlying the eastern Indian Ocean. As a result, the Austral-Indian plate dips under Southeast Asia to form two twitchy fault lines, one splitting the island of Sumatra and the other — the eventual source of the Aceh quake — offshore to the west. At the point offshore where the heavy, grinding plates first meet, they become locked together, such that the diving Austral-India plate drags down the front lip of Southeast Asia, bending it under like a sheet of metal. Sooner or later, the friction grows too great and the Southeast Asia plate, all of a sudden, recoils back into its flat, original position in a giant seismic spasm. This type of megathrust fault also lies off Japan, the northwest of North

America and South America's west coast, and with Sumatra they constitute the most dangerous earthquake sources to people on the jagged circle of faults and volcanoes that envelope the Pacific Ocean: the Ring of Fire.

The theory that explained all of this was known as plate tectonics. It holds that the earth's top crust was formed of about a dozen major — and many minor — interlocking plates that expand from mid-ocean ridges and collide at boundaries like those around the Ring of Fire. The theory was widely accepted by the time Sieh set out for Indonesia. But scant research had been done on Sumatra and researchers did not know the local characteristics of the faults, including the speed at which the Austral-Indian and Southeast Asia plates were colliding, which could be used to infer how often the area produced big earthquakes.

After arriving for the first time in Indonesia, Sieh was reading scientific papers beside a public pool one day in the hot, smoggy capital of Jakarta when he came upon something startling in the works of University of Texas geologist Fred Taylor. Working on the Pacific island of Vanuatu, Taylor had found old corals that had been killed when historic earthquakes lifted them above the low tide mark. Taylor's team had used a new dating technique specialized for corals to place the organisms' death — and the earthquakes — to within a few years of the actual event. Sieh's afternoon went from lazy to electric. Off Sumatra, he had heard of a string of coral reef-encircled islands that sat directly over the offshore fault line. It's the only place in the world where corals sit over an explosive megathrust. "In these islands, you could ride right on the back of the beast during big earthquakes," he says. With Taylor's coral approach, he might be able to get a sense of how this big fault

SURROUNDED

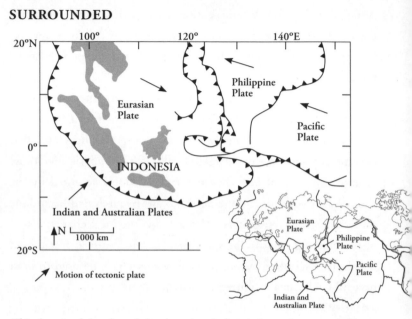

This close up of plate boundaries shows how Indonesia is nearly surrounded by these active seismic zones. (Credited to UNESCO Jakarta)

SLIDING SLABS

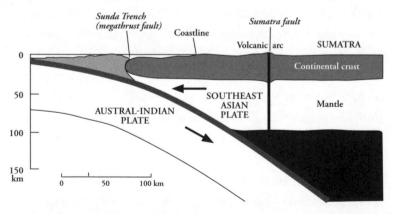

Sliding slabs *In a side view of the meeting of plates at Sumatra, the heavier Austral-India plate, left, slides under Southeast Asia, right.*

behaved, and within his lifetime. "I had my method, and with the islands, I had my location."

Sieh enlisted Taylor in July and August of 1993 and with an Indonesian collaborator they set out to find coral heads on the islands of Nias and the Mentawai chain, where a recent published survey of historical records showed big earthquakes in 1861 and 1833. Sieh suffered quick initiation to island research — he developed painful lumps on his head from smacking the low roof timbers of the local fishing boats they rented. And that summer the team only secured small book-sized samples of coral, won after hours of skull-rattling hammering and chiseling.

So the next summer, when they returned to the Mentawai Island chain, Taylor brought along a chainsaw that building contractors used to cut concrete blocks underwater. Now, the scientists could extract long sections of coral a few meters across, while preserving the integrity of the slice like a finely cut piece of cake.

The slices revealed faint gray and white bands across the inner surface of the corals, similar to a tree's rings. And the bands could be used to recreate history. In the two most common corals in the islands — the cabbage-shaped *Porites* and *Goniastrea* genera — these bands are formed by the organism's new growth in each rainy and dry season. By dating a plug drilled from one ring, the scientists could age the coral. Counting the rings from the date out to the last one at the outer edge of the coral allowed them to see when it died. Or, they could count the years to pronounced curls and knobs on the coral and find out when it went through drastic changes in its shape.

Here, as in Vanuatu, the scientists were guessing that earthquakes actually morphed the corals to create these shapes.

The corals need to be bathed in seawater for their outermost growth cells to survive, so they won't grow much higher than the low tide mark. When a coral is uplifted in an earthquake, and the top portion of the coral head dies, the organism reacts by springing a new outer layer of growth from its sides, below the low tide mark. Between earthquakes, the ground under the coral slowly begins to sink, as it is pulled down with the diving tectonic plate it sits on. The water depth above the coral will increase, and the new budding section of coral will begin to curl upward. When the land and corals sunk enough and there is enough water over the top of the organism again, the outer coral layer will grow up past the original top of the coral head. Now you have a coral head whose changes in form track the movement of the land and the history of the fault under it.

A big enough earthquake will thrust a coral high and dry, killing it completely. Sieh and Co. hunted for those corals on beaches and shallows. The oldest monuments had been blackened by algae and weathered away on the outside but their calcium-infused skeleton tended to hold up over centuries. The best ones also showed outer ridges that would give the scientists evidence of years of sinking before their killer quake. "We just kept looking for that cup shape," Sieh says.

In early 1996, Taylor and one of Sieh's doctoral students homed in on an area in the southern Mentawai Islands that previous researchers sketched as central to the 1833 earthquake. Sure enough, when they dated the corals from a handful of sites their deaths seemed to cluster around the year of the quake. With a few exceptions, the margin of error hung in the five to 10-year range.

Sieh and his colleagues now used the corals to estimate how

CORAL GROWTH PATTERN

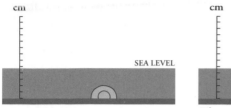 

The coral begins to grow from the sea bottom.

The coral grows up to top sea level, around low tide.

Sea level changes as the coral and land below it are thrust up in an earthquake. The top of coral head dies off and new growth begins below sea level from the sides of the organism.

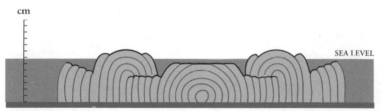

Through many uplifts and sinking cycles, the sea level changes, and so does the height of the coral. This creates peaks and valleys in the organism.

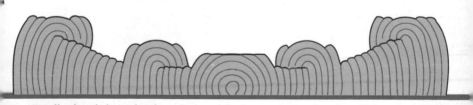

Finally, the whole coral is thrust high and dry by a major earthquake, which can raise islands and corals as much as three meters in Sumatra.

(Images credited to California Institute of Technology, Tectonics Observatory)

much total surface of the islands and seafloor had been uplifted in the quake, making a sort of elevation map using the different samples they'd found. Elevation near the probable center of the earthquake had reached two meters. Just outside that area, corals apparently thrust up a meter. That's a massive amount of movement on the islands, and it portended something bigger down on the underground fault. The oceanic plate only descends under Southeast Asia at a very soft angle, roughly 12 degrees, in the area of the islands. Most of the movement on the fault line during an earthquake there is actually horizontal. Way down at the probable depth of the quake,

This coral on the shore of Simeulue Island, off northern Sumatra, was lifted above the tideline by the massive earthquake in December 2004. (Photo by Kerry Sieh)

40 kilometers below the surface, Southeast Asia would have to slide 13 meters along that gradual incline in an earthquake to pop the islands up a meter or two on the surface. The earthquake would have expended the energy of close to 4 trillion kilowatt hours, slightly more than the energy consumed by the entire United States in one month. In the terms used by geologists, it would have been a quake between magnitude 8.8 and 9.2. A whopper.

But several of the biggest dead corals of the early collections, including one old grandfather head measuring four meters across, didn't date to 1833. They died decades earlier. At first, the scientists thought these were outliers that couldn't be tied to a particular event. But the closer they looked, the more many of these corals seemed to point to an evening in February 1797 chronicled by Dutch officials 150 kilometers away from the islands, in Padang.

***

Padang had just a few thousand people clustered around the Arau River mouth at the south end of the city then. They rode the vicissitudes of the pepper, coffee, cinnamon and gold trades, and that year the place had fallen into recession. The Dutch-led trading group in town feuded with the gold suppliers and these middlemen, based on routes to mines in the Bukit Barisan range, had attacked the city. The Dutch royal family had also recently handed over political control to the British, in the hopes of keeping it out of the hands of Napoleon, then marauding in Europe.

Then around 10 pm on February 10, the earth began to shake. As the rumbling grew stronger, people fled from their homes to an area just north of the settlements along the river, stepping over

cracks in the ground up to 10 centimeters wide. Soon after —
accounts aren't clear how long — three successive tsunami waves
came up the river. One wave lifted a 150-ton English trading
vessel from the river mouth to the bird market behind the old
Dutch fort, more than a kilometer upriver. Smaller wooden canoes
called *perahus* shot another kilometer further upstream to land
in the main market. An outbuilding from the Dutch compound
also washed into the Chinese neighborhood near the fort. People
escaped to trees in the rural seaside village of Air Manis, south of
Padang, only to drown up in the branches. With enough water to
carry the ship, and waves high enough to reach into tree branches,
scientists figure the tsunami topped five meters.

Powerful aftershocks continued in Padang through the night,
and the next day, Padang residents woke up to a settlement
where nearly every building had been damaged. And the physical
stature of the town certainly took a while to recover. A swampy
area developed behind the old Dutch fort and locals rebuilt their
houses on coconut palm stilts, presumably to lift them above
mud flats and debris left by the retreating tsunami.

By the next year, however, English merchants were exporting
coffee from Padang. The population, boosted by the return
of Dutch government officials and soldiers in 1819, swelled to
around 12,000 by 1830. The Dutch army, headquartered at a
new fort north of town, was busy fighting against purist Islamists
and other local forces. Meanwhile, Chinese merchants also
took over the prime riverfront areas of the old Dutch fort along
the riverbank.

That means they were unfortunately placed to receive the
brunt of a second tsunami, which arrived on the heels of the 1833

quake on the night of November 24. This time people headed for higher ground as the earthquake rumbled into a second and, reportedly, third minute. "The entire population of Padang was afoot," Dutch administrator James du Puy wrote. They remembered, says du Puy, the onrushing river of 1797. The river did empty out and return with tsunami waves, but this time they only carried tons of freshwater fish that had been sucked out of the river into the retreating ocean, killed by the high salt concentrations and then deposited on the beach by the tsunami surge. Only one person and two cows lost their lives. But new brick houses in town suffered badly. Some fell over altogether and others developed long cracks in the walls. A church, also of brick, was totaled. Ships moored in Pariaman's harbor, to the north, all ended up onshore. South of Padang, closer to the offshore epicenter, a woman and her child were carried away by the waves at Indrapura and more people drowned at the near-shore island of Pulau Cinto. Four hundred kilometers south in Bencoolen — modern-day Bengkulu — waves wiped out the British customs house in the harbor. And in the highlands near Bencoolen, on the slopes of the volcano Kaba, a previous landslide that had formed a temporary lake was loosened by the quake. The resultant flash flood tore through local villages, killing at least 90 people. Further to the east, rebellious Riau warriors took the earthquake as a sign to attack and sack a Dutch fort.

But after the bricks were picked up in Padang, the city's body politic emerged unscathed. The Dutch army based in the city finally subdued the local forces in the highlands and then ratcheted up the coffee trade there. An urban building boom begun just before the second earthquake continued apace, with some of the old swamps drained by new canals, gridded roads laid down north of the old city by forced laborers and a new gravel-lined path built into the highlands to smooth trade. Travelers to Padang reported well-built houses and new neighborhoods cropping up next to freshly cleared roads. Memory of the earthquake and tsunami all but disappeared under the crunch of gravel in the growing city.

As James du Puy sat down to write up the experiences for publication in the mid-1840s, he would also have noticed how locals made mention of an earthquake forty years earlier that had been more powerful than either of the recent ones — likely one that struck in 1756. Farther back in the annals of his colleagues who'd manned the city were the notes of an army commander, who was helping the Dutch East India Company establish Padang as a foothold in Sumatra and wrest dominance of the west coast gold trade from Acehnese sea captains. An earthquake in 1691 destroyed three stone arches in the commander's house. Six years later, another heavy quake and aftershocks shook the city for 14 days. If anybody cared to notice, earthquakes and tsunamis colored the whole Dutch tenure so far in Padang. And a pattern had developed, of bucking up, rebuilding and moving on with life as quickly as possible.

***

In the Mentawai Islands in the late 1990s, Kerry Sieh and his team could see that the region was accelerating toward some new upheaval. Beaches throughout the island chain were gradually eroding as the ocean's waves lapped higher and higher. Longtime residents described islets disappearing. Barren, dead hardwood trees sat out in tidal shallows. At one spot on the island of Siberut, at the north end of the Mentawais, the researchers found an entire tableau of beachfront life sitting under a meter of water at high tide. Pilings that had once supported a boardwalk now sat submerged near root balls from what had once been a coconut grove. At a spring tide during a lunar eclipse one year in northern Nias, they saw the road to a major wharf disappear under ten centimeters of water. This wasn't climate-induced sea level rise: the islands were sinking. They were being pulled down towards the fault line, as the Australia-Indian plate dragged under the lip of Southeast Asia. Every year in this sinking phase, with the two plates grinding together, was another year closer to the day when Southeast Asia couldn't stand the grinding any more.

A long record of many earthquakes could bring the scientists closer to saying how often they had hit and how soon the next one might come. And Sieh and his team were starting to collect corals killed in the 1600s and even the 1300s: a 1,000-year record of past quakes looked possible.

His main collaborator now was Danny Natawidjaja, a beguiling, doe-eyed Sundanese man who'd grown up in West Java and earned a master's degree in New Zealand. He was one of the few Indonesian geologists interested in pursuing work outside the lucrative petroleum and mining sectors. He met Sieh at a conference in Jakarta in the early 1990s, and later joined Caltech as a doctoral student.

In 2002 and 2003, Sieh and Natawidjaja began to sample heavily at sites where they could obviously see several groups of corals that died in earthquakes previous to 1833 and 1797. They found three places on the Mentawai coast that appeared to have an unusually good collection of these generations of dead corals. At one of the villages called Bulasat, the fault seemed to tip its hat to the crew: a living palm tree on the beach near their sample site fell over after their first day of work there, another victim of rising water levels on the sinking islands.

There were so many apparent age groups of old corals there that Natawidjaja thought at first glance he had found all the 'missing links' dating back through more than 2,000 years of major earthquakes. The record wasn't that perfect. When they dated the Bulasat samples back in the United States, the oldest sample skipped a few generations of quakes and dated to 250 BC. At another village, two different elevations of coral turned out to be of the same era: some had settled lower during the earthquake shaking in more recent years.

But when all the small, drilled-out plugs of coral from each of these three areas came back from dating, a sketch of historic uplifts and possible earthquakes began to fill in. "All the big Eureka! moments do happen in the lab," Natawidjaja says. Some of Bulasat's corals had uplifted in 1347, give or take 18 years. The next site had risen in 1381, plus or minus 9. A third place in 1374, plus or minus 16. There was a gap in dates and then another era of dead corals dated to around 1607 in Bulasat, and to roughly 1613 at the second site, and in 1596, give or take a decade, at the third site. Corals from other reefs rounded out the picture of large earthquakes in about 1350 and 1380, and then a break before the fault resumed remarkable activity first in about 1606 and again in about 1685. During almost all the events, the islands rose at least a meter. The older dead corals also showed decades of sinking before the sudden uplift and earthquake. Smoothing out some of the irregularities in dates, the scientists could see a pattern of rising and falling — big events followed by quiet periods — that extended back to the beginning of the Ming Dynasty.

***

By 2003, it had been 170 years since the last big rupture in 1833. Looking back at the average time between big earthquakes through the last eight centuries offshore in the Mentawais, Sieh and Natawidjaja saw that they tended to hit about every 200 years. It occurred to the scientists that few of the islanders, much less the scientific community, knew about this apparently violent history. Sieh had grown attached to the islands over the years. He'd picked durian with village kids there and slept on the floors of stilted houses. He'd ridden in longboats with fishermen and practiced his choppy Indonesian. In Bulasat, the team had curried favor by fixing the generator that powered village lights. He decided he needed to try to tell the people they were working among what his team was discovering.

"We'd met a lot of people out there," he says. "I felt like if we go on our merry way now and do our science and a tsunami comes along and kills half these people, I wouldn't be surprised if when we returned to the islands the other half killed us."

Sieh's an avid translator of science for the public and over the years he'd grown adept at talking to reporters and curious visitors at Caltech. After an earthquake centered in suburban Los Angeles shook the city in 1994, he and colleagues kept the press rapt with reports about previously unknown faults whose quakes might rip through downtown Los Angeles with similar ferocity in the near future. And he'd developed all sorts of metaphors for talking about faults — loaded springs, elephants on diving boards, sleeping dogs. But Mentawai life is extremely simple and local education rarely runs past elementary school. The team had so far struggled to explain what they were doing, much less learning. "So many people thought we were out on the reefs just to dynamite fish and steal them," Natawidjaja says.

In the spring of 2004, a graphic designer helped Sieh and Natawidjaja put together a poster headlined with the most tangible element of fault movement: "Our Islands are Sinking." In six panels, it explained how evidence from tidal marks on coral reefs and from the growing network of Global Positioning System units in the islands indicated the fault was pulling down on the island — an indication that stress was building for an earthquake. It showed how the sudden rupture of the fault had sprung the islands up in past earthquakes and produced tsunami, and how the fault might do both again. And it suggested running to high ground after a heavy earthquake, in case of tsunami. The poster also recommended building with light wood materials, which Mentawaians often abandoned for concrete as they moved up the economic chain. There wasn't any mention of the region being overdue for a big quake. But the implication was: *Be vigilant*.

With the help of a locally-born Mentawaian anthropology student, Sieh and Natawidjaja and their team passed out the posters at schools and village offices over a three-week Sumatran field mission to the islands in late July and early August 2004. At night, the group put on a show using a makeshift movie screen. In one village, it was on the squat football field in front of the concrete school block. In another, they followed the talk with

Finding Nemo, even as local teenagers called for something with a Hollywood-style gunfight.

People mobbed the movies, snapped up most of the 500 posters Natawidjaja had printed and hung them on the outside of their houses and their shops. But they mostly passed the message by. "I think it was a curious thing that they fought over, but I don't think they paid much attention to us," Sieh says. The few people who did bother to look over the panels brushed them off as fantasy. "Later, the folks in (the Mentawai capital) Tuapejat and other towns told us they thought we were crazy," Natawidjaja says.

At one point that summer, Sieh and Natawidjaja took a ferry back to Padang, on the Sumatran mainland, to meet with the director of the city's planning agency for the first time, and later in the day, with provincial planners. They shared with Sieh and Natawidjaja a startling fact: in the city of 800,000 people, roughly 200,000 lived within one kilometer of the ocean. Padang officials broached the idea of the scientists briefing about 30 local bureaucrats on the new hazards in early December, during the government's annual planning period. But they later wrote to Sieh and told him they didn't have the money to organize the training, nor to fly him back to Padang from the United States. They had other things to pay for.

5.
Not that Bad?

In the post-Aceh tsunami era, however, leaders of the newly formed group Kogami joined with Sieh to develop a map of the city that outlined who in those beachside communities was at the highest risk. They highlighted in red all the areas under five meters in elevation, which Sieh figured had been flooded by the 1797 tsunami.

And then with limited resources, Patra Dewi and her colleagues focused on the more than 250 schools in that 'red zone'. They targeted young people because they had a captive audience, limited resources and support from teachers. But children have also proven to be a key lynchpin in changing a culture's opinion and perspective on new threats and hazards.

The volunteers took to teaching the natural signs of a potential tsunami-generating quake. If an earthquake lasted longer than a minute, people couldn't stand up and many buildings ended up broken, evacuate to high ground, the kids were told. In a city so packed in along the coast, they couldn't take the time to confirm a tsunami was happening. Don't climb into cars. Don't get on a motorcycle. Just get out.

Kogami's trainers reached out to educate taxi drivers, and began discussions with neighborhood leaders. Some of it was trial and error. "I'm embarrassed thinking about back then," Patra Dewi says. "We didn't really know what we were doing. But we had to do something fast." Their enthusiasm and the fact that they were stepping into an education void earned Kogami the attention of international groups and the UN, who began to fund their activities. Eventually, they'd latch onto a rich, cartoon-aided program for kids developed by an environmental group in Bali.

Meanwhile, foreign officials charged with helping people use the developing tsunami warning system approached Patra and Kogami hoping for assistance. Kogami leaders replied that they'd prefer to spend their time on education about natural signs. "I told them 'We don't want people waiting 10 minutes for information'," Patra says. "The scientists tell us we don't have that much time."

Then, just as the group was finding its legs, the earth began to quake in West Sumatra. It started at ten minutes after six in the evening on September 12, 2007, off the city of Bengkulu, with a full 100 seconds of shaking.

Padang suffered a weaker jolt, but it still stunned the place briefly. Much of the city was heading to sundown prayers to begin the fasting month of Ramadan. Mayor Fauzi Bahar received a text message from Jakarta's meteorological and geophysical department that the undersea earthquake was shallow enough and strong enough to generate a tsunami. The nascent tsunami warning system was getting its first test. Within 15 minutes of the quake, Fauzi announced the threat on the local channel of Radio Republik

Indonesia, the national radio station, as four TV stations began to broadcast the bulletin as well. All over the city people were getting the message. And they didn't know quite what to do with it. They continued to stream out on the north-south routes, as well as head for the hills on the east-west roads — people were as interested in continuing home to their families, with the first Ramadan prayers on their minds, as they were in evacuating to higher ground. A follow-up survey of 200 people living in the red zone by the water found that of the 70% who heard the warning through the radio, television, neighbors, or, in a few cases, through mosque or community loudspeakers, only a quarter chose to at least leave the beach area or climb up a tall building.

The tsunami did come to Padang, but it was only a benign half-meter high, sweeping in the Arau River and past the decaying row of colonial buildings on shore there about 30 minutes after the quake. North of Bengkulu, the waves reached four meters high but rural villagers all managed to escape them.

But the fault wasn't done. Early the next morning, a second pulse originated under the Mentawai Islands opposite Padang, far closer than the previous night's shake.

People woke to see things moving that had never defied inertia before. In a neighborhood just east of downtown, Australian Kirk Willcox's bedside lamp and flower vases leapt off their perches. Near the beach area, radio station owner Aim Zein's 30-meter transmission tower jerked back and forth like a whip. Up in the hillside neighborhood near the city's cement plant, where power cables slithered loose of their poles, one man ran out onto his street with his neighbors and looked back at his house to see the windows flexing in and out, like they were laughing at him.

At her home, Patra Dewi climbed into a blue sports utility vehicle with her parents and crossed the Kuranji River near a large shopping mall, which now had a long vertical crack down much of its five-story façade. Whereas her group had tried to keep it simple in their trainings — walk, don't drive to avoid traffic jams — the stickier points of evacuating, such as moving an old or infirm person in a flash, were just becoming clear. Patra's mother has osteoporosis and can't walk very well. So on they drove, onto what is normally one of the busiest thoroughfares in the city. Luckily people hadn't taken to their vehicles yet that morning, and the family rolled easily toward safety near the local hill, Gunung Pangilun. "There's another route to high ground but my parents thought it would be bottlenecked. I had to listen to my parents!" Patra says, noting the strong pull of Indonesian family protocol even for a 34-year-old. "We should never have crossed the bridge. What if it was damaged in the earthquake or a tsunami was coming?"

Patra wasn't the only one improvising. Aim Zein, the radio station owner and a consultant with German technicians building up the tsunami early warning system, stayed put in his house-cum-radio station (the latter is attached to the former), one kilometer from the beach. He built a little escape ladder to his roof and cleared a path through a broken wall to the two-story school next door. And soon after, he started up live on one of his two channels.

"I thought, 'There are not so many buildings collapsed. These people out there are like me; they need instructions.'" His wife would not leave either with their small son — even though Aim urged her to go east of the beach with friends. Instead, she came on the radio as well. One of their instructions: if you live near the beach, go as high as possible.

Twenty-five people died throughout Western Sumatra, while some 50,000 homes and structures were damaged. After the Aceh tragedy, however, and a related quake in Nias Island that killed 1,300, another deadly tsunami in Java in 2006 and a devastating quake in the cultural capital of Yogyakarta that same year, this was a mild inconvenience in Indonesian terms. A few dozen families lingered at makeshift camps in an old Chinese graveyard up on the ridgeline south of the Arau River. The panic of 2005 was replaced by more calm and composure. In the absence of deeply felt lessons about how to respond to a heavy earthquake or a clear directive over the radio, people had thought for themselves. They had overwhelmingly decided a tsunami was not coming or, if it was, that they'd face it on their own turf. Many chose a family member's house or the mosque instead of high ground, afraid of fighting the crowds or traffic or any other unknowns outside their area. People told surveyors and journalists afterward that they'd been on *waspada* — 'alert'.

But was the city simply lucky or had scientists overstated the risk? The two linked earthquakes, an 8.4 followed by a 7.9, had exploded with a fraction of the power Sieh and Natawidjaja had guessed was unleashed in either of the 1833 and 1797 quakes. The scientists were at a loss as to why the 2007 pair hadn't combined and spread across a wider area to replicate the size of even one of those historic events, which might have jacked up a bigger tsunami and sent it straight to Padang. And the area under the northern Mentawai Islands that had appeared to be most poised for a big earthquake didn't slip much at all during these September quakes.

To some, the fault looked like it might behave differently in this cycle of quakes. Irish seismologist John McCloskey, a close student of the Sumatran megathrust fault, said he thought the risk of a quake as big as the magnitude 9 of 1833 had diminished significantly. When he appeared later before the Padang city legislature with Patra, he emphasized a range of potential tsunami waves that could hit the city now, many far below the five meters Sieh and Natawidjaja estimated for historical tsunamis in Padang.

In similar areas around the Pacific Rim, where written history and sediment research show cycles of big earthquakes on these undersea megathrust faults, they behave differently from cycle to cycle. Sometimes they will release in one mega quake, sometimes in a couple of merely large events. Records stretch back 1,300 years at the Nankai Trough fault, which sits off southern Honshu, Japan, and caused some of the devastating tsunamis that tore through the island. The last three cycles show a magnitude 8.6 earthquake across a broad expanse of the fault there in 1707, two 8.4s rupturing smaller areas in 1854, and then an 8.0 followed by a 7.9 in the mid 1940s.

This idea had the potential to lessen the urgency education groups could bring to the city. Sieh and McCloskey met and decided scientists should speak with one voice in saying a substantial risk of big earthquake and tsunami remained under the Mentawai Islands. What all the scientists knew was that the earth's crust is elastic. However much one piece of that crust is bent as the two plates collide between earthquake cycles, it will eventually spring back the same amount as the plates pull apart during earthquakes. And when Sieh and his colleagues looked at the amount of movement during the 2007 quakes, compared to the amount of bending Southeast Asia had been doing over the last two centuries, they found there was still a lot of action waiting to happen. They calculated that just one fourth of the pressure that had built up over the last quiet period had been relieved in 2007. Enough potential energy for a high magnitude 8 quake was still sitting in those areas where the plates were locked up.

6.
Deep in the Pit

Tsunamis begin insidiously, to the naked eye. An earthquake-rocked ocean floor pushes such a huge volume of water that they cross the open ocean like a layer or a fast moving tide. In series or in singles, they may be 500 kilometers from one crest to the next in deep water. A fishing boat will barely feel that sort of wave's gentle rise or fall. That's why the Japanese named it a strange 'harbor wave'. It doesn't bare its face in the deep ocean for the fishermen to see, like the big wind waves that fishermen often battle.

When the giant earthquake struck 90 kilometers off the coast of Aceh on the morning of December 26, 2004, it levered a patch of ocean floor the size of Tasmania one to three meters up into the water column. More of this uplift continued north along the fault, into the Andaman Islands. Then every place west of the line — India, Sri Lanka, the Maldives, Somalia — first saw a surge of water from this disturbance. To the east of the tilt, along the beaches west of Banda Aceh, water drained into a depression created by the earthquake just offshore. It exposed the coral reefs that nobody had ever seen dry, and a muddy bottom strewn with hundreds of fish flapping and gasping for air. Then, that huge area of uplifted water farther out to sea came running downhill toward Sumatra at the speed of a jet airliner.

It announced its arrival 20 minutes later with the crushing, rumbling sound of exploding munitions. It could have been the sound of the earth's crust cracking and adjusting at the tail end

The famous, animated 'Great Wave Off Kanagawa' print by Japanese artist Hokusai has been used as a tsunami logo the world over, although most scientists think he was only depicting a storm wave. Into the late 1990s, the United Nations International Tsunami Information Center used the wave in its insignia. And visitors can still get a T-shirt with Hokusai's wave on it at the Pacific Tsunami Museum in Hilo, Hawaii. (Courtesy of Earthquake Engineering Laboratory, UC Berkeley)

of the earthquake, or the sound of the water colliding with outer islands. In any case, the surges of rushing water hit shallower bottom as they approached Banda Aceh, slowed to around 50 kilometers an hour, and stacked up. They began to show a face, even to look something like waves. David Lines, an Australian surfer living with his Acehnese wife and their son on the shallow reefs west of Banda Aceh, at the edge of the golf course, looked with a fleeting sense of attraction at one of the first green-blue walls forming far offshore.

"It was actually barreling. And part of me was going, 'That's not a bad-looking wave'," Lines told a television reporter later. All the same, Lines knew exactly what was going on, he shouldn't wait around to see it break. He hustled the family into their car and drove quickly away from the beach, stopping to pile in a few local women on the way out of the neighborhood. Then, in a moment that seems near impossible but that Lines insists happened, he looked in his rearview mirror and saw one of the first tsunami waves hit the lines of trees along the shore, exploding in a ferocious froth. The size of the initial spray reduced people running behind him to stick figures. Out to sea, one fisherman said the wave's impact at that moment turned everything to smoke.

And there were at least seven more behind.

Lines was able to get to high ground. And he later saved a few people using an inner tube. He said afterward, with the pluck of a surfer who looks out to sea during a tsunami and knows what he's seeing, that the waves and their aftermath had in fact been invigorating. He was able to save people. He got his family out of harm's way. He had a front row seat for all the action.

***

Surfers who willingly charge down the steepest walls of water that form up over the jagged Sumatran reefs are a little bit crazy. They are some of the best of the best — brand-sponsored riders and gutsy amateurs. They come from Chile, Portugal, Brazil, France, all over Australia, Hawaii. (They will leave Hawaii, for this stuff.) And they tend to converge on the sweetest spot in Sumatra: the Mentawai Islands. Here, the waves roll in from the furious, storm-addled Southern Ocean off Antarctica, most consistently from April to October. Aficionados can track the swells at online forecasting sites, as they build and lengthen across nearly 5,000 kilometers of open water. They arrive smooth enough and tall enough to double over into barrels of blue glass and house the visiting surfers standing straight up, their arms held over their heads triumphantly. The dreams of mavericks here tilt toward civilian nightmare: gliding in a giant, endless envelope of Mentawai water. "We're in surf as big as tsunamis every day!" says Matt George, the tsunami relief organizer in Padang in 2005, who's also senior editor at the American magazine *Surfer*, and has been surfing the Mentawais since the mid-1990s.

Charter operators running three dozen boats out of Padang are of this edgy ilk. The industry is built around surfers who visited the offshore islands on a safari and started their business to prolong the adventure. One charter owner I got to know began his love affair with the offshore reefs on hair-brained cruises to empty wave lineups aboard fishing boats in 1997. The experience included a nighttime drift in a rollicking storm off southern Nias, when his rickety boat's engine conked out, and he and fellow surf safarians worked a hand bilge pump and some makeshift sea anchors as waves broke across the beam of the 12-meter ship.

Surf captains understand that any surf adventure gains currency if there's a brush with risk — a storm or two, gymnastic wipeouts, and even a little bloodshed. It's standard fare for someone to open up a foot or a leg after falling down a wave and scraping the barbed reefs. The gaudiest wound is the head gash, which requires quick and strange inverted Mohawk haircuts and then somebody — usually the captain — to take a needle and thread to the affected's scalp. Walking through the airport in Medan or Padang, the shaved and stitched folks look strangely and proudly initiated. Flat days in the islands might bring other sorts of adventure. At a Padang watering hole one night, a Uruguayan captain whipped himself into a sarcastic frenzy over a drunken crew member who, on an idle day, had decided to test his balance on the rails of a dingy that was spinning in a circle with the help of whirring outboard motor. Not content with that feat, the guy tried to back-flip up off the spinning boat and into the water. And this aspiring Greg Louganis planted his shoulder right on the whirling prop. "That guy was one fookin' lucky sonofabitch," Uruguay said. The prop sliced his collarbone cleanly but somehow missed all the crucial arteries. Back to Padang on a speedboat for him. On with the trip for the rest.

Not even terrorists dissuade the hardiest. Another captain in Padang speaks of paying off Kalashnikov-toting Aceh separatists with cash and whisky to gain access to untouched waves there during the conflict years. When deadly bombs tore through two pubs frequented by surfers in Bali in 2002, the purists, in hushed tones, said this would merely thin out the popular Bali waves of the pretenders.

To the adventure mix of late, the earth has added tsunamis.

Nobody really knows what the next tsunami will look like in the Mentawai Islands. The islands are so close to the earthquake source and the surges will probably come quick and messy. The sea bottom doesn't rise uniformly after a shallow earthquake. Instead of a smooth, hydraulic lift, the floor gets rumpled and warped and uneven. When the surges hit an island that sits right near the source, the tsunamis often don't have enough open water to spread and lengthen nor do they hit a long, shallow continental shelf that pushes them up into a destructive wall — what scientists call a bore, of the sort that drilled through villages on mainland Aceh. Still, communities near the source can stare down giant waves because the morphing sea floor nearby is so extreme. On northern Simeulue, 40 kilometers from the 2004 epicenter, the waves quickly rose as high as nine meters high.

An earthquake in March 2005 raised a small islet off Nias Island, near Sumatra, and exposed a band of whitened, dead coral. (Photo by Kerry Sieh)

The rumbling seafloor can also cause underwater landslides, with the most serious repercussions nearby. In 1998, just off the north coast of the island of Papua New Guinea, a moderate magnitude 7 earthquake sent a chunk of seafloor tumbling down an underwater cliff and threw a tsunami surge 15 meters tall at one section of the island. The extreme wave heights, however, were isolated to a collection of towns and cities spanning 30 kilometers along the coast. The waves barely registered by the time they crossed the Pacific to Japan. More subtly, in September 2007, a localized patch of uplift just off a bay in the northern Mentawais sent a one-meter tsunami up a river, to a small village where it flooded residents' porches. Other villagers on the same bay didn't even get their feet wet.

Islands close to the source may get a break: the earthquake can raise them up one or two meters, pulling wide expanses of coral reef above high tide and forming a new tsunami breakwater. This happened in Nias after a 2005 earthquake. On the other hand, the earthquake also dragged parts of northeastern Nias downward, exposing villages there not only to the small tsunamis but to inundations during every high tide thereafter.

So in the future, the Mentawais could be looking at a benign tsunami. Or a terrifying one. They could get swirling, sucking, strange tide-like movements. Or a five-meter wave homing in on the bays where the surfers hang out. They will know as soon as ten minutes after the earthquake.

In private, the more conscientious surf operators do worry.

"It's basically like having a grenade tied around your neck by a delicate string," one operator says. "You don't know when the string will snap."

Another says, "I would never want to be quoted on this but I've been scared every day I've been here."

But nobody is willing to walk away from the best waves in the world, and the money to be made from ferrying people to them.

***

A few weeks after the twin earthquakes gave that near miss to West Sumatra, in September 2007, I find Australian-born charter boat operator Chris Scurrah hurrying back and forth through the Batang Arau Hotel along Padang's Arau River, readying a surfing charter docked in the river for an imminent Mentawai Island departure. The hotel's back patio has a new gash down the center from the quakes' shaking, but features a familiar mid-morning scene: Western surfing tourists and boat crews gathering, bleary-eyed, for breakfast or the next string of rum-and-cokes. Some are coming down from the island surfing high; others are gearing up for it. Down on the river below the aged fortress of the 'Bat' — a converted 1908 Dutch bank building — wooden fishing launches roll in and out of the estuary. The Gado-Gado hillside rises steeply opposite, peppered with houses hidden by rain trees, cinnamon, bamboo and the odd palm.

Scurrah's had no cancellations since the quake for the three boats he runs, and 10 surfers are waiting to board a psychedelic blue ship of his. "I was getting emails from customers overseas asking what kind of AC adapters the boat has and I'm thinking 'My God, people, the earth is moving here'," says Scurrah's sassy American partner Christina Fowler, who's 40, wears black-rimmed, vintage eyeglasses, runs the hotel and helps out with the surf business.

The fault, meanwhile, continues to add new twists to surf tourism life. After reefs uplifted during the September quakes, a famous wave called Macaroni's at the southern end of the Mentawais looked to Scurrah to have shortened when he surfed it. A report from another charter operator in the region claimed that raised reefs further south had eliminated another surf break known as Rags Right. At least two surfers had opened up serious gashes from striking their heads on underwater reefs at Macaroni's since the earthquake, including one boat cook who knew the waves well.

"Why are our most experienced guys getting injured — that's the question," says the scruffy, blonde, gentle-voiced Scurrah, 33, known as 'Scuzz' around the hotel. He and Fowler have taken to sleeping with an upside down beer bottle on the floor of the bedroom — a crude alarm that clanks over in an earthquake. She's convinced him to wear shoes and socks in preparation for an evacuation. They know this is not an isolated incident. They have hosted Kerry Sieh on the patio many times and voraciously read the science press. They speak fluently about island sinking and uplift cycles. An updated tsunami map by California tsunami modeler Jose Borrero, which shows a potential flood of five meters here along the river, enjoys a prominent spot near the cash register in the soaring lobby of the hotel.

Still, customers on the patio insist that they did message Scurrah and Fowler after the earthquake to ask if everything was OK, and when it came time for the owners to blink, they did not. *Come*, the customers were told. The visitors have stopped to think — at least briefly — what they're getting themselves into. One young Californian, already well versed on the wallop waiting on the San Andreas Fault back home, says he's "only got one life", and turns quickly back to his eggs. Nearby, a South African father of two has been eyeing the Padang tsunami flood map, and running the odds a little more carefully. On the one hand, the tourist's exceptionalism reigns: it's only two weeks out of a lifetime. "I figure we're on land for two days and the rest of the time we'll be moored in deep water, so the risk is minor," he says. "But I don't want to be eating my words in a few days." There are the people who depend on the tourism dollars to think about, as well. After the Aceh tsunami, the foreign surfers were also encouraged to come back here. And they did. Staying home, says the South African, "just leads to people's demise sooner."

When I stop by briefly to visit with the surfers out at sea, the meter-and-a-half waves and sun have pretty much consumed any worries. A second Californian, who also took some time out to distribute relief supplies to island villages that had been cut off and even damaged in the recent quakes, says, "This morning we were sitting there on the charter boat talking about waves and it was like nothing had changed. Out on the water, I really don't think about anything else."

Scurrah's decided he can't afford to relax in the islands. He confesses to sleeping on pins and needles when he spends the night anchored in some shallow bays that might channel a tsunami. And he's become convinced that Nias' south-facing bays were scoured by historical tsunamis coming north from the Mentawais. As a result, he orders his captains to anchor away from those exposed bays at night in Nias and the smaller Telos and Hinakos chains, where his boats often go to avoid crowded Mentawai breaks during the high season.

When he goes for a jog on flat stretches of island sand, he

envisions hustling across the coral and swimming out to sea to avoid the tsunami's wrath on land. In the wave lineup with clients, Scurrah sometimes tells them they would need to paddle out to deeper water if they felt a big earthquake. The boat, he says, will be cutting anchor and heading out to sea.

Nearly everybody in the business sees deep water as the safety zone, far away from those 'harbor waves'.

And deep water is even the refuge of choice for purveyors of the newest version of Mentawai surf tourism — up-market land resorts, where guests pay $200 a night to live in understated thatched roof villas equipped with Jacuzzis and satellite internet and programming, so one doesn't have to miss an English Premier League match even though you're castaway on a sandbar in the Indian Ocean. Some owners here imagine piling into launches — typically used to ferry customers around to different surf spots — to get quickly to deep water after a quake. But it's a smoothly-operated system that will hustle guests down to the beach, kick-start the launch motors, pile everyone in and get out to deep water ahead of receding tides in a matter of minutes. At Macaroni's resort, hard by the famous wave of the same name in the southern Mentawais, owner Mark Loughran has the added challenge of being on a palm-fringed islet surrounded by shallow lagoons.

When the tsunami hit in 2004, reflecting from Aceh off Africa and back into his spot with one-meter waves late in the day, Loughran was just starting construction. He'd been at the project for years. He first got to know the area by living with a family in a village on a nearby estuary and canoeing out to the break each morning. He'd spent almost two years negotiating with local villagers for the resort land, and used some of his grandfather's

Macaroni's Resort in the Mentawai Islands. (Photo by Jeffri Adriyanto)

inheritance and money from family and friends back in Australia to get the project going.

So as workers prepared to drive in a meter-and-half thick steel pole to anchor his bar and restaurant a few days later, Loughran told them: dig in deeper. He wasn't giving up Maca's. He finished the thatched-roofed, open-sided bar and restaurant rotunda with flexible timbers set in concrete blocks and bracketed to the blocks with steel. He then began piecing together his own picture of a future tsunami. He trawled YouTube for video of how the 2004 tsunami arrived on barrier reef islands like the Maldives, south of the Indian subcontinent. Most of the shots from islands looked like rivers spilling across their banks, not walls of terrifying water. Later, he read about the reefs that uplifted in the great earthquake on Nias and southern Simeulue in 2005, and finally, watched the ground rise 30 centimeters out his back door during the 2007 quakes.

"I think we'll get about a one- or two-meter tsunami in the future. The thing will just come through here and blow out the windows and flow through," says Loughran, while pulling his blond bangs behind his ears one morning outside the restaurant. He plans to be on the third floor watching it all go down, and has installed an alarm so he can summon guests to the restaurant, as well. "They tend to come to the bar whenever there's an earthquake," he says.

As Loughran talks on the morning I visit him, a handful of sunscreen streaked surfers mow through their breaded fish lunch in the restaurant, yapping happily between bites and riding the emotional lift from a morning in the waves. They've already checked photos of themselves from yesterday's surf session, posted on the resort webpage. All around them is a warm, aqua and green wash of mangrove trees and coconut palms and crystal clear water. One staff member is pulling young coconuts from a tree, poking holes in the top and offering them up to drink. When the surfers' dreams of Mentawai tube riding finish up, they finish in a place like this. "This has been the trip of a lifetime and I've been coming to Indo since I was nine years old," says a 49-year-old currency trader from Perth. He seems to be not so much walking as floating around in his flip-flops, a slight smirk plastered on his face. When he hears the talk of tsunamis, his expression changes very little. He looks out to the lagoon and says, "Don't think I'd like to be here for a tsunami."

"Third floor, mate," Loughran says, hurriedly. "Third floor."

Not everyone believes the resort and its occupants will get off easily. One of those shallow bays where Chris Scurrah tends to sleep restlessly is right here at Macaroni's. The U-shaped bay at Macaroni's could channel tsunamis toward the back of it and amplify their height, says tsunami modeler Jose Borrero, himself a frequenter of Mentawai surf breaks. (For the record, he doubts paddling a surfboard safely to sea is possible.)

Other escape plans in the islands have kinks in them. The owners of another resort, at the north end of the Mentawais, have added a bridge across a mangrove-lined tidal flat to a high ridgeline that rises to 50 meters behind their resort. The hill feels safe above the beautiful but vulnerable beachside bungalows. But the bridge, made from rough-hewn timbers and planks stuck in the mud, doesn't look like a match for a grisly earthquake, and the flat sucks like quick sand. Borrero agrees that the tsunami bridge may not stand through a heavy quake. But the owners called up and conferred with him as they were mulling escape scenarios and this seemed like the best option. "At least they've got a plan," Borrero says.

Indeed, it would be easy to write these guys off as adrenaline-hungry yahoos and miss how attuned to the elements they are every day, and how much they've thought about tsunamis. They spend their lives reading the tides and the wind and skies to routinely find the best waves and skirt storms. Many were spending the off-season in Malaysia and Thailand in December 2004, where they saw what was developing and managed to get out of danger during that tsunami. And there's a sense among captains — rightfully so — that the most experienced would similarly read the signs of a future tsunami and react quicker than anyone else.

The margin they live on is too hair-thin for me. But these are surfers. When they allow themselves to be drawn into the hollow of a tubular wave, they say they are in the pit. The deeper in the pit you go, the more you risk being buried in the wash of the wave. All the same, being deep in the pit is that rush every surfer lives for. And the best know how to keep from getting in too deep.

7.
The Balance Point

In mid-2008, Padang Mayor Fauzi Bahar, facing re-election later in the year, seems to be talking out of the many sides of his mouth. In one sense, he's grabbing the tsunami bull by the horns. His support for Kogami has grown and the city is now funding some of the group's education work in schools. Patra Dewi no longer has to vet all her teaching materials and handouts through the city officials. The city has a rough evacuation plan developed with Kogami's help, and the government has explored land purchases to widen some of the few roads that lead east from downtown. The mayor's office has held meetings to discuss vertical escape towers, which would allow people in beachside communities to quickly climb above a tsunami flood, and various government and university groups are also identifying tall buildings — hotels, malls, bank offices — that could be used for escapes. There's even new rock berms reinforcing the beach (although these were of little deterrence to the Aceh tsunami).

At the same time, Fauzi has also announced a partnership with

Dutch developers to expand the city's waterfront footprint, with a new resort, an expanded port south of the city and a tunnel to connect the developments to another larger port and natural gas storage facility further to the south. Seemingly undaunted by the tsunami and earthquake risks, Fauzi tells news reporters that the tunnel will be built to withstand a "10 on the Richter scale".

Meanwhile, the mayor has placed billboards along the main road into Padang from the north, with two story-high pictures of himself and written maxims that encourage locals to pray and do good works in order to avoid disaster. One roughly translates to 'If you don't want to invite disaster, don't do bad things'. Another reads 'If we repeat the 99 Holy Names, [Allah's exalted monikers] God will protect us from disaster'.

I chomp at the bit, trying to figure out how all these ventures and ideas can hang together. "Maybe you should ask him," Patra says, unruffled.

To get to Fauzi, I'm first vetted by Agung, a charming aide with smooth English who, on the night we meet, is also courting a delegation from Padang's German sister city, Hildesheim, hoping to solicit some investment in the waterfront projects. Agung's also fluent in the language of disasters, having networked with Kogami and foreign groups about preparing the city for earthquakes and tsunami. "It's difficult to be 100% ready," he says. "We learn the signs of tsunami. And we also have this thing called *pasrah* in Indonesia. Submit to the will of God. Many people here believe in that."

Pasrah follows the popular Sunni Muslim belief that the span of your life is already known when you are born. A Hadith proclaimed by the Prophet Muhammad explains that the first thing God created was a pen, and he told the pen *Write everything that is and will be.*

"From the day you are born, God determines how long your life is," Agung says. "Tomorrow you could be dead in your sleep. But even if you subscribe to *pasrah*, it's the last resort. You have to take precaution."

After several tries Agung arranges a semi-appointment with Fauzi during evening visiting hours at the mayor's house, a modest but well-appointed one-story neocolonial on a tree-lined avenue that hosts an upscale Pizza Hut restaurant and an English language center where wealthy families send their kids. After an hour or so of waiting, Agung and I enter the inner chambers to meet Fauzi, who looks small, narrow shouldered and bleary-eyed as it approaches 9 pm — a contrast to the pressed, gleaming mayor with a close cropped mustache who always graces billboards and TV clips. But he greets me with a hearty handshake and looks me silently in the eye as Agung explains we've come to talk about tsunamis and local economics.

Following a career in the military, Fauzi, 46, won his seat in 2003 after losing the vote count but convincing friendly factions in the national house of representatives to overturn the result and give him the office, on account that his opponent's vice mayor candidate falsified parts of his resume. In 2005, Fauzi began pushing through several conservative laws in the city, including requirements that school girls wear ankle-length clothing and headscarves and that unmarried women not be allowed out at night alone.

In his receiving room, lined with baroque-looking couches, we sit through an impromptu pitch from a cell service salesman hoping to upgrade the Mayor's plan. The coffee table we're perched around is actually a glassed-in case, with a scaled model of all the planned waterfront projects, right down to the five-star hotel on the old

Chinese cemetery at the mouth of the Arau River. Dispatching the salesman, Fauzi leans in over the model to explain his economic strategy, with the aide of a PowerPoint presentation that Agung has cued up on a laptop.

There is greater export potential here — crude palm oil, natural gas, cement from the local factory — if the ports can be expanded. "The port is so important to prevent people from becoming scared about the tsunami," Fauzi says, with Agung translating. "I'm trying to make this area an economic center."

He skips on quickly to a video on a different laptop, punctuated by school kids running along the road during a series of earthquake and tsunami drills. Fauzi says they're doing this every month, although Patra later claims the schools are not practicing anywhere near that frequently. ("It's really hard to get them to do drills," she says.) In the continuing footage, Fauzi announces the start of a 2005 tsunami drill on the anniversary of the Aceh disaster.

"In the past few years I've taken my own initiative — I risked my life to tell people about the dangers. And getting the word out about disasters, it's become S.O.P." — standard operating procedure. He reminds me that right after the first earthquake in September 2007, he went to Radio Republik Indonesia offices down the street to tell people about tsunami warning, before calling it off.

"That's risky," I allow.

"Yeah, we're just a few hundred meters from the ocean," he says.

Striding through to the next room, he sends Agung scurrying to turn on an overhead light to illuminate a picture of himself in his green Navy Seal dress uniform. "The wings there on my uniform are from Australia, for underwater demolition exercises," he says.

He's not scared of floods, he continues, spreading an indestructible smile across his face. "I can survive."

"Why do people need to pray?" I say, hoping to catch him quickly out of depth, flexing his survivalist muscles.

He turns to Agung, "He's seen the billboards?"

Agung nods.

"It will give people in town a peaceful feeling so they aren't fearful," Fauzi says to me.

When we go back into the sitting room, Fauzi keeps walking out another door toward the residential part of the house, telling Agung he hasn't had a shower all day. My ten minutes are up.

Agung tries to clarify the mayor's approach to danger by using an analogy of a car left in a parking lot — first you lock, and if thieves get in after that, well, *pasrah*. "From the Mayor's point of view, all Muslims think like that," Agung says.

***

Fauzi is not highly regarded among the business and academic elite in Padang, especially when it comes to pulling off his plans on the waterfront. Aim Zein, the radio station owner who has his own political ambitions in town, says, "I'll pray for him on the waterfront development. But he doesn't even have capability to manage transport next to his own office" — where minibuses are in a constant jam that Fauzi has long promised to relieve.

"Those are going to have to be some big strong buildings to withstand an earthquake and serve as tsunami escapes on fill land," says Febrin Ismail, the Andalas engineering professor and Kogami advisor. Journalists and students grumble about Fauzi's backroom dealings to secure his first election; they're also neutered by fear of his military connections, and won't rally behind any opposition. Some clerics felt uncomfortable with his push for mass prayers in a downtown city park after Aceh.

But he's also ahead in polls. And I've never heard anybody call him contradictory. In West Sumatra, his ideas don't necessarily cancel each other out. They will be hotly debated, but they are allowed to coexist. That's because the region's response to ever-encroaching modernity has been to synthesize opposing ideas. It aims to be a big, discordant tent.

Many anthropologists and historians studying West Sumatra, led by the Bukittinggi-born, Cornell University-educated Taufik Abdullah, hold that inherent tensions color the basic cultural building blocks of the Minangkabau, who represent 80% of the region's population. "In Minangkabau, the concept of conflict is not only recognized but is institutionalized within the social system itself. Conflict is… essential to achieving the integration of the society," Abdullah wrote in a seminal paper in 1966.

The struggles begin in the traditional home, where the biological father attends to the needs of his wife and his children in a house where he's often treated like an outsider. At the same time, he's also burdened by the affairs of his sister's house and children — his responsibility under the mandates of a matrilineal system in which inheritance runs through the mother. In the historical legend of the Minangkabau, peace between these two competing maternal and paternal strains in the society is modeled in the way the people set up an early political system: there was a monarchy led by kings, but also strong village councils led by matrilineal clan heads.

Islam provided perhaps the greatest challenge to the

Minangkabau sense of balance in the early 1800s, when Wahhabi reformists returning from Arabia brought a new male-centric moral code to the Minang highlands. Islam had been around for three centuries but had never been as radicalized as the version that the turbaned, bearded *hajjis* brewed in new walled religious compounds in the region. They targeted matrilineal customs — *adat* — and also grew in stature by eliminating corruption and patronage to facilitate and benefit from a boom in regional coffee trade. The conflict grew nasty and bloody at times, with the Islamists (known as Padris) murdering clan chiefs, burning traditional houses and killing the royal family in 1815.

A popular account holds that the Dutch entered the struggle on behalf of the traditionalists in 1821, and after 15 years of intermittent fighting, subdued the Padris and their leader, Imam Bondjol. But there's a twist to the storyline. Bondjol had a remarkable change of heart in 1833, when he sought to reconcile with matrilineal chiefs — "I will live in mutual respect and peace and no longer will I meddle in the lives of *adat* leaders," Bondjol wrote in a memoir. The two sides then united to struggle against the Dutch for three more years, before Bondjol was smoked out in a siege of his highland compound and then sent into exile.

The long-term effect of the war, says historian Jeffrey Hadler, was a new accommodation of Islam by the traditionalists. Written versions of the Minang history appeared for the first time after the war and strengthened the place of Islamic moral teachings that had been folded into local culture. In practical life, Islam helped create space for individual property, even land, owned by men and women, alongside the system of traditional lands passed down through one's mother's line. Still, proverbs surviving to this day place the life-giving strength of nature — undeniably maternal — at the center of Minang culture: the Minang say 'Growth in nature is our teacher'.

Accommodating Islam set the tone for absorbing other modern ideas. Around the turn of the century, the Minang blossomed intellectually in the growing ranks of Dutch and Islamic schools in the area and from new forays to Javanese universities. In Padang, the intellectuals opened dozens of newspapers and magazines, and made it the publishing capital of all of the Dutch East Indies. The pages were electrified by worldwide currents of communism, reformist Islam and feminism. West Sumatra chaffed under the Dutch, staging an uprising against new taxes in 1908, and an outburst led by communists and coal miners in the city of Sawahlunto in 1926. Minang thinkers in the Indies, like writer and future government minister Muhammad Yamin, and those in the Netherlands, such as future vice president Muhammad Hatta, began to agitate for a united Indonesian state. West Sumatran students in Java dissolved their Sumatran organization and eventually pledged to the idea of one national state in the Youth Pledge of 1928, a landmark moment in Indonesia's independence movement.

While Hadler suggests this passionate embrace, and creative formation, of new ideas was born of the healthy conflict between Islam and matriarchy, Taufik Abdullah attributes it the Minang custom of young men traveling out of the homeland in search of fortune — known as *merantau*. Today, there are legion Minang traders and small business people in ports all across Indonesia, and *merantau* remains powerful in Minangkabau thought.

"We have an expression, 'Wherever you are, stand on the earth and hold up the sky'," says Febrin Ismail of Andalas University.

"We're sort of like Singapore in that we have good human resources."

Success, however, doesn't mean losing your Minang roots. "When you're successful on the outside, you come back," Febrin says. It's typical to see fortunate businessmen come back to build impressive traditional family homes in their ancestral villages in the Minang highlands. And like the rest of Indonesia's Muslims, most Minang travel to their family villages during the annual Idul Fitri celebrations at the end of Ramadan, re-affirming age-old tensions and accommodations by celebrating a holiday born of a patriarchal religion on their mother's home ground.

***

In the 1750s, Europe and America had both their beliefs and the ground underfoot rocked profoundly by large earthquakes. While London and New England suffered a series of quakes that knocked chimneys off their perch and opened up a few water geysers, Lisbon, Portugal endured a harrowing shake on the morning of November 1, 1755, that scientists now place in the range of a magnitude 8.7. Most of the Catholic city was in church on this All Saints' Day, and in three massive shocks, nearly all the houses of worship collapsed, burying a lot of the faithful there. People who managed to run outside into open space along the banks of the Tagus River, which winds through the heart of the city, were washed away a few minutes later by giant tsunami waves. At one point, a chasm opened up along one of the waterfront wharfs and swallowed people and ships whole. A horrendous fire followed, started by candles and cook stoves, and it burned for five days, gutting the downtown. All over coastal Portugal, southwestern Spain and North Africa, cities and towns faced towering tsunami waves of up to 30 meters. The final death toll probably reached 70,000. And the shaking from the quake carried all the way to Finland.

The drama of Lisbon in 1755 gave artists — and thinkers — plenty of material. (Courtesy of Earthquake Engineering Laboratory, UC Berkeley)

When the dust cleared, philosophers and preachers all over Europe started a hot debate about the presence of a divine power in the horrors of Lisbon. European thinkers had just emerged from an era that had invented the word 'optimism', and they had gone to great lengths to prove that God was benevolent and his good intentions could be found even amongst the evil in the world. But after Lisbon this attitude came under attack. No less than the legendary French writer and philosopher Voltaire wrote that if intellectuals had told the injured survivors "'… your particular misfortune is nothing, it contributes to the universal good', such a harangue would doubtless have been as cruel as the earthquake was fatal." Meanwhile, academics — many of them also ordained priests in the Christian universities — set out to explain the earthquakes in the rational, earthly new language developing among learned people of the day: science. Some tested the idea that earthquakes could be triggered by irregularities in the weather, either by calm stillness or alternatively, by lightning and storms. A newer theory, based on phenomena observed during recent earthquakes, suggested that fires deep within the earth caused steam vapors to expand the earth's surface and trigger the quakes. They were off, by the measure of today's scientific knowledge, but the gathering of sensory clues in papers and pamphlets published in London and elsewhere was convincing enough that religious leaders felt threatened. Attributing the earthquakes to natural phenomena was nonsense, they retorted. "First case, it is untrue; secondly, it is uncomfortable," wrote one outspoken English priest. Instead, he wrote that God was likely punishing sinful Lisbon, where the Church had been sponsoring the Inquisition court aimed at ferreting out non-believers and punishing them savagely; probably He was making an "inquisition for blood… if so, it is not surprising He should begin there, where so much blood has been poured on the ground like water."

The debate raged on about whether a benevolent God or even an ordered universe He set into motion could possibly explain natural disasters. The struggle formed the heart of Voltaire's classic work, *Candide*, about characters wrestling with the meaning of hardship. The worth of tangible nature overshadowed a seemingly capricious God in that book.

Today, the West is still living in the aftermath of that debate, in which science seems to have won. Scientific explanations of natural events hold sway — especially in the media — over a vocal minority of believers in divine intervention, who are treated as folksy and entertaining at best. Scientists steer clear of engaging in a debate about the role of religion in natural disaster. Christian charity groups pour in to clean up in disasters' aftermath without any suggestion that something other than physics was at work.

But other cultures, including Islamic-influenced ones, are taking a different view. It's not either/or, it's "theologically heterogeneous", as David Chester, an English volcanologist and Christian minister, puts it. Finding the right balance of science and religion has been a hot topic in Indonesia, spilling onto the radio airwaves, the opinion pages of the local newspapers and discussion threads on Facebook. After the Aceh tsunami and the series of smaller earthquakes in early 2005, followed by the arousal of a dozen volcanoes in the archipelago, an unnerved citizen sent President Yudhoyono a text message asking him to slaughter 1,000 goats to appease whatever Furies were causing the upheavals. "Don't be superstitious," Yudhoyono said in public statements, responding to the text. "There's a scientific explanation for this series of earthquakes," added the president, who holds a doctorate in agricultural economics. But he also let his 88% Muslim country know that he was holding daily prayer meetings to ask for protection from God.

The challenge for people like Yudhoyono is to get people to buy into the science of earthquakes, tsunamis and volcanoes by nesting the science tightly enough in religious belief to lower people's risk.

***

On a cool, misty July day in 2009, I bump along in a Toyota utility vehicle toward the town of Solok, in the Minang highlands, with Buya Mas'oed Abidin, the former head of West Sumatra's top clerics (the Ulama Council) and one of the province's most admired thinkers. Abidin is 75, with drawn cheeks and a light brown prayer cap atop his head. He studied at religious schools and universities in Sumatra and Malaysia, but was also deeply formed by joining early nation building efforts and rubbing shoulders with theologians and statesmen through various conferences and organizations in the 1950s and 1960s, including Malik Ahmad, once a leader of Muhammadiyah, Indonesia's second largest Muslim group. "These guys had the principle to serve country and party," he says. "When they spoke, they were talking about Lincoln and Washington. Ahmad could recite the Gettysburg address."

This afternoon, Abidin is scheduled to make the closing speech on mental preparedness at a local conference on disaster. This area of the highlands is no stranger to natural hazards — a March 2007 magnitude 6.4 quake on the mainland Sumatra fault was centered just 35 kilometers north of Solok and killed 70 people in the surrounding district. While driving through Solok, Abidin ties much of local problems with disaster to all the latent messages of the rural landscape that seem to have been lost. "When I was a child," he says, remembering his upbringing a few hours north of here, "whenever there was a big rain and big waves formed on the river, people knew there was a flood coming. They'd prohibit children from going to the river and get ready to go up high. Nowadays, this doesn't happen." Rolling through the clusters of houses along the rice paddies, he points out that despite their vaulting rooflines shaped like buffalo horns, the homes are all one story and built of wood, "Look at how they anticipate the earthquakes." As we pass the fog-enshrouded and still-active volcanic cone of Mount Talang, he says, "Usually the animals will come down from the mountain when it's about to blow. Danger has a sign." He's beginning to sound like a sun-wrinkled farmer.

Arriving at the meeting hall of the local vocational college, we find an audience of teachers, community organizers, and khaki-clad government bureaucrats bored stiff from listening to two national meteorology and geophysical agency staff explain the flow of information in the event of a disaster in the province. In the back rows, the gang has lapsed into chatting and smoking cigarettes. But a few minutes later, Abidin, necklaced with a white *hajji* scarf, snaps them to attention: 'Return to God', reads his first slide, translated. Now, when he mentions the traditional knowledge of animals coming down off a restive volcano, there's no mistaking where the knowledge originates: "The Quran says that everything comes from God," he says.

As the talk unfolds, a rhythm develops: Quranic verse, followed by traditional wisdom, then a new verse. *When seawater is made to flood and graves are torn open then each soul will know what he's done and what he's neglected.* Abidin: "Kids used to know how to make emergency coffins out of wood, now they wait for body bags." *When God loves a nation he will test it many times.* Abidin: "When we were little, we used to treat wounds with cassava leaves." To the proverb-loving Minang, this is sweet-sounding poetry.

At the same time, Abidin urges the crowd to seek knowledge

— it's compulsory for every good Muslim from birth to death. "It's imperative to combine our ancestors' tradition with technology and with faith. I'm urging everybody to do that anywhere and anytime in life," he says.

The crowd, including this observer, grows rapt. When Abidin nonchalantly slides in a joke — "Technology cannot always tell everything: even with ultrasound how can we know if it's a girlish boy or a boyish girl?" — they double over in laughter. They nod approvingly at his interpretation of the scriptures. One man interrupts to ask for a copy of the show. Abidin has an overriding calmness about him, an ethereal earthiness. He is actually getting people to sit here in the waning afternoon and listen to a philosophy of disaster. The anthropologist Taufik Abdullah says the Minang cleave to something that balances appropriateness, possibility and divine truth. Here is a version in the flesh.

The ultimate mental pirouette comes when Abidin shows a slide bearing a geologist's view of Sumatra's offshore fault, with the Austral-Indian plate diving under Sumatra, next to a Quranic verse, translated to: *When the Earth is stretched and casts forth what is in it, then the Earth is hollow and it obeys its God as it must.*

"It is true that an earthquake is because of nature's efforts to balance itself," Abidin says. "But there's also the effect of the will of God at work. In West Sumatra, we've long been seen as a potential disaster area. But the Big One hasn't hit yet. I don't mean to be prejudiced in our favor. But let's say it's possible that we have a quake but no tsunami."

"Reciting prayers," he says, "might just prevent disaster."

Back in the car, I push on this idea some more, by asking Masni Fanshuri, a law student who's traveling with us as a translator, to mention a sermon he heard in a mosque about eight months ago. City officials were discussing new escape routes in town, and a particular *imam* he heard suggested that building the new routes or using them to run away in the face of a tsunami revealed a lack of faith. Instead, people should stay put and pray.

Abidin wags his finger and shakes his head at the mention of this. "This is absolutely mistaken," he says. "Faith without science is misleading and people tend to follow those who are mistaken about this. I've made my views known to the Ulama Council about this. We need to move our hands and Allah will lead the way. You need to do something in this situation."

Passing back by Mount Talang, now revealing its dark, lava-domed summit, he says, "It's the science that harnesses the faith and the faith that harnesses the science." At another moment he adds, "Nature isn't formed randomly, it comes from something. In all faiths, this comes from God. It's not impossible to connect science and faith. It's a must." Just before we part ways, he spells out his Facebook address. Ulama in Java had recently questioned whether or not the networking site was *haram*, or unholy, suggesting it led youth astray by allowing them to court and swap pictures online. "The rules of *haram* come from God," Abidin says, brushing off the Javanese. Besides, he loved chatting with followers on his site.

***

Back in Padang, Patra Dewi, who is also the devout head of the women's guild in her mosque, is treading the fearless, compelling middle ground that Buya Abidin has mapped out.

"God doesn't control the earthquake but he can help us," she says. "But if we're not prepared at all, that's bad."

This idea of a productive partnership between Kogami and God gains her traction in the region, including in mosques on the coast north of Padang, in the area around the shrine of the province's first proselytizer, dating to the 16th century. After seven months of Kogami outreach there, Patra and colleagues leave such a strong impression that one mosque agrees to build a tsunami escape platform into the third floor of its redesigned building.

Closer to home, the lecturers and bureaucrats in her neighborhood of Air Tawar Barat gather one night to hear the Kogami road show in the modest Air Tawar mosque, with its open sides, wood-paneled ceiling and small metallic dome. Gesturing in front of a video projection, Mohon, Kogami's chief presenter, spends a half-hour explaining how the megathrust works, the need for evacuation plans and how it's the heavy earthquakes that send a tsunami, usually within 30 minutes of the initial shaking. Afterward, the crowd, three-dozen strong and scattered throughout the building on their prayer mats, peppers Mohon with questions. How is it, an elderly man asks, that one of the 2007 earthquakes lasted longer than a minute and there was no tsunami? Mohon shifts from foot-to-foot and says it was too deep to cause one. Won't the outer islands always protect us? asks another man. "No," says Mohon quickly. A woman wants to know if a long, rolling quake or a quick, vertical shaking will more likely cause a tsunami. "Don't start that," Mohon says. "You can't tell." Their inquisitiveness has caught even the local experts off guard, and the idea that science can't totally explain tsunamis hangs in the air.

Mohon and Patra join the neat lines of people — men up

front, white-cloaked women behind a curtain in back — and the group prostrates toward the west for the final prayer of the day. Afterward, one of the questioners seems grateful for the show. "We've got the same situation as Aceh: I'm 200 meters from the ocean," he says, adding that he's also got one bad leg that limits his speed on the ground. "I think, based on today, that I'll teach my family to run right after the quake to a high area about 1.5 kilometers from here."

Some of the wealthy living along the coast, including those in a neighborhood just across the river from Air Tawar, could amortize a new house up high after Aceh. But most of the middle class folks here can't afford a move to shiny new developments uphill (some of them advertised as being 'tsunami-safe') or to older tracts with climbing price tags around the cement factory. And they certainly can't duplicate the quiet charm of the *kampung* in Air Tawar Barat — with its narrow lanes, scraggly gardens, and the cool wash of the sea breeze day and night. Patra admits that it will be tough to make an escape with her parents if the narrow bridges across the cobblestone canal separating her house from the mainland give way in a quake. "But I could never get this somewhere else," she says one evening as the setting sun turns the village's rusted tin roofs a deep cayenne, and we stand near the mosque and watch students stroll home along the canal. The bats begin to work over the waterway. A cycle taxi carrying a young woman in its canopied seat rolls by. As the *muezzin*'s throaty, elegiac call wafts out from the turret loudspeaker, she goes off for a well-worn ritual in a familiar place.

Faith is still considered the strongest weapon when living so close to the ocean. 'We believe in God', is what I hear again and again

volunteered to go and coordinate things. He arrived a few days after the tsunami struck and spent a month there. What he saw causes him to shiver reflexively as he talks about it. "I thought I was very *berani* — brave. But I was scared. I couldn't eat for the first week. So many bodies, everything was broken and it looked like everyone went crazy."

The moment that seems scariest now, more than four years later, was the time when a dazed man walked up to Arya in Banda Aceh and asked if he knew where the bank was. No, Arya replied. "I had a lot of money in there and I need it right now!" the man said angrily. There was a pause and then he asked, "Have you found my child?" Arya's baby was just under a year old at that point. When he returned to Padang, he began hearing that the city's offshore geology was eerily similar to Aceh's. And he began to see himself wandering around in another disaster wasteland, this time looking for his own child. "I am human. I want to see my kid grow up. What could happen if I was away and I lived through it and the baby didn't? I couldn't handle that. I'm not scared of dying in a tsunami. I'm scared of afterward."

He tried to absorb all the latest science to understand when and where a tsunami might strike. He discovered Kogami and followed closely the information it gave out. But after the near-miss of the 2007 earthquakes, scientific explanations seemed not to be telling the whole story.

"BMG [the meteorological and geophysical agency] said the tsunami potential was there!" he says. "So what's happening? You have to find a mix between knowledge and something else."

Unfortunately for Arya, that 'something' isn't comforting; it keeps him constantly guessing. While watching television in

December of 2007, he saw the news of a hoax earthquake and tsunami prediction for December 24 flash by on the news ticker, followed closely by a government reminder that these things can't be predicted. But he convinced his family to go on a vacation to the resort island of Batam near Singapore, disguising it as a Christmas getaway. "I didn't tell them," he says. Few other people in Padang responded to the hoax.

While we talk, there's another tsunami hoax in the air. This one has been spreading through email and warns of calamity around an upcoming solar eclipse. Kerry Sieh has addressed this, I say. The other day Sieh told a Singapore TV station that there is absolutely no connection between eclipses and earthquakes. Arya seems to latch on to that explanation.

But two months later when I find him again in Padang, just after the eclipse, he acts like I abandoned him: "Where were you?" he shouts. He had asked his family to go for an overnight to Bukittinggi, the highland getaway at 930 meters above sea level. But Arya's wife sniffed out the cause, and although she agreed to go anyway, they decided only to take their child out of school for two days, as a precaution.

His fellow Padangans have found a way to mix science and the supernatural. But the mix can sometimes be lethal, even for a good Muslim like Arya.

"It's complicated," he says.

So twisted, in fact, that I can't contain exasperated laughs sometimes when he's explaining himself.

"You can't understand. You need to live here," he shoots back. Then he gets feisty, knowing how candid he's being. "Twenty-five million for each answer," he says, as I keep probing.

Eventually I suggest he see a therapist, "This has gone way beyond rational."

"They do it like that in Jakarta," he says, dismissing help.

He is pursuing other jobs far away from Padang, although he'd like to stay with his company in Indonesia. "Borneo is the only island of the largest six that isn't dangerous," he says.

"Pontianak's nice," he says, thinking of the city on Borneo's west coast. "Why not Pontianak?"

***

Mayor Fauzi, however, is with the balanced. A few weeks before the mayoral election in late 2008, he sensed that there wasn't much more to say right now. The billboards asking people to pray to avoid disaster came down. New signs with Fauzi and his smiling, prayer-capped candidate for vice mayor went up in their place. They promised *Religius* (Devotion), *Ikhlas* (Sincerity), *Tegas* (Clarity), *Merakyat* (Populism). In an hour-long televised debate not long before election day, he and the four other candidates managed to avoid ever saying the words 'Tsunami', 'Earthquake' or 'Disaster'. It didn't seem to matter that nothing of the waterfront development materialized, and the escape building and roads plan is foundering. Fauzi promised new things: waived school fees and free books for students, free rice for the poor and a new health insurance program. And he played it right: he won overwhelmingly, snaring 50% of the vote.

8.

A Longhouse on the Hill

In the Mentawai Islands, people are living in a different orbit. Word comes slowly from the islands that a growing number of villages there are actually picking up and moving permanently following the shakes in September 2007 and heavy aftershocks that continued the next year. They range from the large town of Malakopa at the southern end of the islands, where the government helped a town of 300 families relocate to a hill behind their original settlement — after every house was shaken to the ground in the earthquakes — to smaller hamlets that have reshuffled their housing plans on their existing footprints. Is it just that they're closer and fearfully riding the fault's every movement, or is there something inherent in the islanders that's compelling them to be more proactive?

In July of 2009, I gather translator Jeffri Adriyanto, a 21-year-old Padang English student and hitch a ride to the islands on the *KM Andalas*, the wooden cargo ship that Danny Natawidjaja and Sieh have refitted for research in recent years. Natawidjaja and a crew from the Earth Observatory of Singapore, Sieh's new research center, are venturing out to download data from the team's global positioning system stations in their tucked away Mentawai hillocks. All aboard, we rock 16 hours from Padang, through seas nicked by flocks of scattering flying fish, past the glaring spotlights of the Padang fishing fleet to the star-painted skies behind, before drifting below Sipora and down the west coast of the island of North Pagai. We drop anchor near Macaroni's surf break, where the 2007 quakes shook hard and raised surrounding reefs. Sieh had also heard a story, passed down through local villagers, of an historic quake — probably the one in 1833 — that lifted reefs out of the water here.

From the lee of a small island, ringed in coral sand beaches and coconut palms, we pack into a small rubber dingy with six scientists and boat hands and motor up a narrow, mangrove-lined river towards the nearby village of Silabu. Nervous jokes fly about the crocodiles people have seen in the swamp here, and the old trees baring their gnarly roots in the twilight look like they're about to take foot. We pass a hand-painted signpost stuck in the mud: *DON'T PANIC EVACUATION ROUTE*, it says in Indonesian, and points upriver (it had floated down from the village in a flash flood). Natawidjaja says, "Silabu's pretty safe from the tsunami, so far up the river with all these mangroves to protect them." An old woman in a rattan hat paddles a dugout silently past.

More than a kilometer upstream, the boat noses into a muddy bank and we slither past a pigsty built over the river. Natawidjaja and his crew go off to the GPS station on the hill behind the village and Jeffri and I amble up narrow footpaths between wooden bungalows on stilts, parting the clumps of barefoot, curious kids and scrawny chickens, in search of the village headman Demas Sakerebau's house.

With little introduction from us, Demas' son-in-law ushers us into the back of the spare brick-and-cement home, still the most ornate in the village, not least because it has a wooden bed frame in one room — the room offered up to us. When Demas and his daughter return

The Mentawai Islands — *Siberut, Sipora, North Pagai and South Pagai. The line to the west marks the point where the Austral-Indian plate starts its dive under Southeast Asia.*

from a two-hour motorbike journey from the market in Sikakap, she feeds us eggs and chili sauce over rice. Afterwards, Demas fires up the gas generator and lights his house like a Christmas tree in the midst of darkening Silabu. People draw in to sit on his slab floor and watch his TV and we settle in on the front patio with the lively village secretary, Amerson, listening to him talk between pulls on clove-spiced *kretek* cigarettes.

In June 2000, on a day that seems eons ago, a magnitude 7.9 quake struck undersea to the southwest of the Mentawais, about 325 kilometers from Silabu. The shaking rang an iron bell up in a tower in the old wooden church, which sat across the path from Demas' house, in a space used now for volleyball. "We stayed in our houses throughout the quake," Amerson says. "We didn't feel any sense of panic. But that's a pretty strong shake to ring that thing — *Kong! Kong!*"

Everything changed after Aceh. When Amerson says the word repeatedly, he widens his eyes and pounds a fist against his heart. One thousand kilometers south, here in Silabu, the reverberating waves from the Aceh quake caused the local river to drain to mud, then slowly fill in, an ebbing and flowing that continued throughout the day. Then, news of Aceh's floating cars and bodies ripped across the airwaves. Amerson watched a few YouTube clips down at Mark Loughran's surf resort, where he worked as a security guard during 2006 and 2007. But instead of making things look manageable, as they had to Loughran, the online images only increased the anxiety. Amerson remembers distinctly watching the way downtown Banda Aceh's streets turned quickly into a torrent in video shots, and also how the Aceh River over spilled its banks. A closer quake might cause a tsunami to tear up the river and through Silabu, just as it had in Banda Aceh, Amerson reckoned. "They experienced the river rising there in Aceh and our houses are on the same sort of flat land here," he says.

The earthquakes of September 2007 damaged 90% of the houses here, including Amerson's. (You can hear wooden frames snapping on a video a development worker took of the second quake here.) The wooden church's bell tower came down in the first quake and the building was finished off in the second. Afterward, Amerson took to sleeping on the hill behind the town with his family and other fretful villagers, next to the same global positioning unit that a villager once told Sieh he'd brought with divine guidance.

With so much damage and so many shaky nerves, it was an opportune time to rethink the whole settlement. Demas and other

School kids in the Mentawai village of Silabu.

village leaders explored a plan to move the village — all 150 houses — up behind their refuge hill. But the high cost to bring equipment to clear and flatten the land proved prohibitive. Instead, Amerson and about 50 other families in the village decided to rebuild away from the banks of the small river and closer to the base of their hill — which is about 10 meters high.

He, his wife and their three kids stayed in a tent at their new site for about six months, while he and some relatives put together a boxy, stilted bungalow with a thatch roof, smaller than his last place and all paid for out of his own pocket. Silabu's rebuilding money promised by the Mentawai district government had still not arrived when we visited, and some worry it's already been 'eaten' by bureaucrats at the district capital in Sipora. Amerson was able to save his old TV and some lumber — although not his dish cabinet, one of the family's few pieces of furniture. Meanwhile, villagers had a sturdy new concrete church, built with the help of the Mentawai Protestant community, to worship at on the hill.

***

The next morning when we wake, Demas, a cheery round man with the only pair of glasses I saw in the village, has gathered Amerson and a dozen other sun-leathered men on his kitchen floor to tell the story of the historic quake. Sieh's group's coral samples from around Silabu showed over a meter and a half of uplift movement in the area during the 1833 quake, and now the elders here want to tell their version.

Jago Tiboiet, a wiry 70-year-old with wisps of a goatee on his chin, chimes in first, under a growing layer of cigarette smoke.

"I don't remember the year exactly," Jago says, "But the island rose up in an earthquake. It was the one we call Silabu Sabeu and the other island next to it. This is according to the ancestors."

"There is also another story," he says, stopping briefly to talk with a friend next to him. "The area around here became beach because the waves came crashing in.

"It happened when we could still drink and wash in the river," he adds. "We stayed out near the rice paddies then and the village here was known as Simabebeguet, which means 'many rattan'," after the plant with strong, palm-like leaves that is used for all kinds of goods around the village.

A younger guy across the circle says that the place eventually changed its name to Silabu because the new island was perfectly round like a pumpkin — *labu* in the Mentawai dialect. "There's no other name to use; it just had to be like that," Jago adds.

"There's a hill not far from here, named Tibalet, which means 'waves crashing onto rocks'," says Jago's elder friend next to him. "There are some corals around the village from that time," someone says. "No, women have used them to build things around the village," another responds.

The powerful, island-forming earthquake and apparent tsunami seem to match up with the uplifted corals scientists found. What's curious is that the people who watched it happen have been scrubbed from the story.

As the men chat rambunctiously over the next half hour or so, veering off here and there to tell a popular history of the village — the customary limits on mangrove use, the way the Japanese had dug trenches all over the area during World War II, the adulterer and Peeping Tom who was excommunicated from the village in the 1970s — they establish that the story of old geologic upheaval is limited to that. Everybody believes it's true; "It's not legend," they keep reminding me. But there are no victims and no flattened homes.

The historical memory of a de-fanged earthquake is akin to the way Silabu thought of earthquakes in the period leading up to Aceh. People considered tremors of any size to be signs of something. If one came in the morning, it was counted as a good omen for fruit trees in the village. Copious harvests were sure to follow, especially on the durian trees. If it came in the evening, an earthquake meant sickness. Somebody would come down with a headache or the flu. This is a legend one hears throughout the Mentawais. Earthquakes could mean bad things but in themselves weren't so dangerous. That's why everybody could stay in their house. "If you had a party and an earthquake happened, you used to continue on with the party," Demas says. "We lost all of that belief after Aceh."

***

As the gathering breaks up, Demas neatly prints the names of the men — Aiannia Sakerebau, Arben Siritoitet, Jago Tiboiet, Lertaminus, Jhonson. Among the traditional Mentawaian sounds, there's a conspicuous dearth of the Christian names you hear a lot around the islands. But Demas assures that everyone has converted. Christianity arrived here in Silabu in 1916, 15 years after the first German Protestant missionary, August Lett, landed in this area of the Mentawais — just about the last frontier for world religions. Lett was killed while trying to settle a dispute between Dutch officials and locals, before the missionaries had converted a single soul. But a deputy of his came and stayed in the area around Silabu and eventually convinced residents, who were living in ancestral houses, that their animism built around shamans called *kerei* was no longer viable. To unmistakably declare a new era of village life, the people burned down their traditional straw and wood houses. And they built bonfires to burn the beaded headdresses, drums and other accoutrements of the *kerei*. "After that there was no *kerei*," Demas says. "Everything that gave them power was burned."

The fires in the islands continued on into the era of a new Indonesian state. Police bent on bringing traditionalists into village life, as part of the official state policy, would force the *kerei* to cover up in clothes, cut their hair and then collect their implements and burn them. People in Siberut, the biggest and most densely forested island at the north end of the chain, held out the longest. Pockets remained of indigenous life, based around longhouses of several families subsisting on sago palm flour, pigs, chickens and the odd primates of the forest — pygmy gibbons and langurs. The traditionalists earned a measure of protection following a flood of environmental activism by local and international groups in the 1980s, the United Nations' declaration of Siberut as a biosphere reserve and finally, President Suharto's abrupt cancellation in 1993 of logging concessions on Siberut and his designation of roughly the western half of the island as a national park. But 97% of islanders became at least nominally Christian. (The Christians allowed the islanders to keep their beloved pigs.) And villages came to dominate the landscape of the islands.

What blew away in the ashes of traditional culture was a sense of the undersea fault's violence, which had once been woven deeply into local stories and taboos. Traditional taboos reflected the tenuous life in the islands, marked as it was by infant death, disease and headhunting from neighboring clans. In traditional belief, a soul will only choose to stay with the body, bound in this life, if it is happy and gets regular attention. A person adds tattoos, files his or her teeth, and performs regular rituals throughout life to continue this binding. And he has to keep good relations with the corresponding souls of everything around him — animals, trees, waterways, metals for household use. So too must the living appease the ancestors, who reside out of sight in remote tracts of forest on small islets and can bring good fortune or bad tidings just like nonhuman spirits.

The medicine men, *kerei*, guided the communications with the spiritual world, and they gained status by long months of seclusion, an elaborate trance-filled initiation and then oral teachings with elders. Sickness is the most common sign of a discordant spirit come to visit, and the *kerei* swoop in to ritualize it away. But contact with the spirit realm can come at any time, for anybody. When Dutch anthropologist Reimar Schefold, considered the dean of Siberut studies, first visited western Siberut in 1967, a young teenager who'd gone missing in the forest returned to his longhouse in a trance, decorated with flowers in his hair and a painted face. He told his family he'd entered a longhouse in the spirit world on the other side, and it was frightfully beautiful. So much so that both he and his family feared his days among the living were numbered. Schefold witnessed an edgy *kerei* initiation ceremony hastily arranged to lure the soul of the boy, Sigilaket, back to this life. "Sigilaket kept tearing himself away from the festivities, running into the forest weeping and singing; he had to be brought back by force. But gradually he calmed down. The other shamans took him into their circle and together they sang the triumphant exaltation of a new *kerei*."

Earthquakes are enmeshed in the constant communication between the present world and spirit world. Even the vestige belief about quakes that survived Christianity's arrival in Silabu and lived right up to Aceh — that quakes were signs of something — signals their totemic power over the living. But that isn't the whole picture, according to traditions that are still kept alive in some areas up north, on the island of Siberut. One branch of lore builds on the powerful spirit of watercourses, who lives at the bottom of rivers and oceans, controls the fruit harvest and can visit sickness or enemies on a village. Once, he appeared in the form of a crocodile to an orphan boy, and showed the boy all the intricacies of building the perfect longhouse. The boy returned to his relatives, who were taking care of him at the time. But as he began to dig the deep hole for the main post of the longhouse, the relatives grew jealous of his new knowledge, and they set upon him and killed him. They threw his body down into the hole. Little did they know that the boy would become a spirit that haunts every house, at the base of the main post. When the earth shakes, it's the angry boy at work. And so is his mentor, the watercourse spirit who can deliver durian or sickness to the longhouse.

In a more tragically Greek-tinted version of earthquake origins, an extended family gathers in festive glee in a valley on the west coast of Siberut, to build a longhouse. They've collected the large timbers for the posts, cut boards for the floor, palms for roofing and rattan for binding ropes. After the postholes are dug, the head of the longhouse throws his chisel down the main posthole, making it look like an accident. He sends his brother-in-law, whom he despises, down to get the tool. And just when the brother-in-law is at the bottom of the pit, he calls the family in to place the main pillar, right on top of the man. The doomed bugger manages a pathetic groan as he's buried alive. But an oblivious, or mostly oblivious, family finishes the longhouse. Then the headman summons all his neighbors and extended relatives and slaughters pigs and chickens for a great feast. Just before they sit to eat, the spirit of the dead man appears to his sister and tells her to take her children outside the longhouse to eat. They wait under a banana tree as the rest of the party gathers around the princely feast to eat in the gleaming new house. Then the spirit unleashes a thundering earthquake from the base of the main post, shaking the longhouse until it collapses on top of the party and kills everyone.

Adherents to this version make offerings to the spirit, loosely called 'grandfather', each time they build a new longhouse. Koen Meyers, who works at the Jakarta office of the United Nations Education, Science and Cultural Organization and who's been collecting Mentawai legends of earthquakes, thinks there may be other references to the 'grandfather' in Mentawai traditional folk tales, including a children's song that mentions animals running amok as an earthquake begins, possibly to get away from a tsunami. Meyers, who's been traveling and working among Siberutans since the early 1990s, thinks the loose term for grandfather is used because, traditionally, people don't want to call the earthquake by its actual name, for fear of rousing it. This is common taboo for the powerful forces that lurk unseen in Mentwaian life. And it betrays a healthy, age-old, familial respect — a fear — for the power that could bring a big, strong longhouse to its knees.

With the dislocation of new religion, the arrival of colonial outposts and resettlement under the Indonesian state, this sort of knowledge becomes blurred. "Now it becomes more difficult to hear stories," Meyers says. "They even get lost in Siberut."

What's also been lost, as Mentawaians have resettled along the coast, is the reason they once lived exclusively upstream, deep in the forest. Anthropologist Reimar Schefold says he first read suggestions that Mentawaians lived off the coast for fear of tsunamis in writings of colonial naturalists, who'd traveled to Siberut in the early 1900s — then, even more than now, home to legion animals and plants found nowhere else on the planet. But in Schefold's four decades of living and studying on Siberut, he was never able to confirm that tsunamis were the cause of forest living habits. Schefold says the easier explanation is that people settled where the river water grew sweet, upstream of the estuaries affected by seawater intrusion. Regardless, Schefold found that deep forest dwellers were deeply suspicious of the sea, hanging back in fear when he traveled to the coast with them.

Meanwhile, more modern villagers up and down the island chain grew adapted to life within earshot of the coast, learning to fish and travel in longboats and build with newfangled — and more brittle — concrete and brick materials. People in the smaller southern islands, where the traditions eroded faster, increasingly moved to the coast to get health care and schooling offered by the Indonesian government. All of this happened in the quiet 50 years preceding Aceh, when tsunamis in the islands were unheard of.

***

Wherever you are in the islands, the hardships of everyday life that gave rise to Mentawai traditional taboos have not faded. Almost everyone seems to sweat to scrape together a livelihood, hauling mounds of patchouli leaves or piles of coconuts from surrounding forests and groves to the village, in order to reduce the raw harvest to oils sold in the port towns and used later in botanicals and foodstuffs. They still raise most of their own food in forest fields, cleared without fire by felling trees and allowing them to rot, compost and fertilize the area. And in the mangroves and local bays, women hunt for prawns with rattan fish traps and the men twirl hand lines out of their dugouts looking for bony, white fish.

Shuttling across a lagoon in North Pagai. (Photo by Jeffri Adriyanto)

Farming and foraging is for everyone, even grandparents. In the mornings, we watch this wrinkled and weathered generation step into their rubber boots, pull on rattan rope packs and leaf hats and tramp out to the fields and swamps. One afternoon we find Amborosius, the man who'd sold his coconut grove to Mark Loughran for the Macaroni's resort, working to put together thatch roof panels in one of Loughran's villas. Ambo, as everyone in Silabu calls him, earned about $10,000 in the sale, but he'd put it aside for one of his grandchildren to use for education. Now, he spends most nights down in the resort dormitory with the young bartenders and surf guides and rises each morning to do maintenance for a wage. "We'll be killed first if there's a tsunami here," he says with a wry, one-toothed smile. "But if we don't work, we don't eat."

Jeffri and I are regularly probed for bandages and painkillers and diarrhea relief pills, and see things get out of hand that would usually be solved with a quick trip to a clinic or dentist in Padang. In one village, a man's left cheek has blown up like a football, from some sort of abscess in his mouth. A friend says the man had seen a doctor at some point but couldn't afford the surgery that had to be done. "He's hopeless about his condition now," the friend says. "Sometimes at night, he's coughing up blood. But he's fine when he goes out to the fields in the morning to work." Malaria and tuberculosis lurk as constant threats. A 2007 survey by the humanitarian group SurfAid, which works in the islands, found that close to one in ten local children die before their fifth birthday. In the most isolated Mentawai villages, the rate is closer to three in ten.

A few modern machines nudge up the standards of living. There are only 3,500 electricity accounts for a population of more than 65,000 and they are overwhelmingly in the island capital. So in the remotest corners, villagers often pool funds to buy a generator (or solicit a donation from a logging company or nonprofit group), string up wires to give each house a few light bulbs worth of illumination,

Elderly women return from the forest at dusk in Silabu. (Photo by Jeffri Adriyanto)

and then collect a couple of dollars per house per month for fuel. A web of formal and informal longboat taxis — hollowed logs propelled by outboard motors — fill in for sparse service from the one ferry that traverses the coast of the 325-kilometer long Mentawai group. (Two other boats serve the mainland.)

Leaving Silabu, with the *Andalas* research boat long gone, we turn to local transport, trying to get north to Sipora. Two village men take us on a slippery forest motorbike ride on rutted tracks through arching groves of tan-barked *abizzia* hardwoods. Some tracts have already been eaten at by loggers but in a dense grove I spy one tree bending heavily under the weight of some primate that rushes quickly out of view. From Sikakap, overlooking the strait between the Pagai islands, we roll gently north on the ferry loaded down with durian and sleeping children and droves of men headed for work on the mainland. Once in a while, longboats bearing women in their best silken pastels flag down the ferry and men hoist them aboard amidst the building south swells. The women belly laugh with relief at staying dry, as they drag their burlap sacks of fruits up onto the ship. After six hours, we see our first jetty and round it into the market town of Sioban, in eastern Sipora.

On the concrete wharf, a nervous, unshaven guy fiddling with the engine on his longboat finally agrees to take us one hour down the coast for the equivalent of $50. (A lurking middleman tries, unsuccessfully, to raise the price further and get a cut of the deal.) Between the easy downwind surf we had on the ferry here, the haggling and some back and forth with Jeffri about how we need to act tough with people on the docks, I lose sight of the fact that the strong southerly breeze has turned the afternoon rotten for longboat travel. And our boat is not up to it.

Soon after we settle onto boards laid across the dugout's bottom, the captain wobbles the narrow craft while peeling out of the harbor and into the swells, throwing up a spray that flies right into Jeffri's eyes and smarts. "I can't see," he cries out. That's when we begin smacking the waves violently, each landing sending a shiver down the frame of the boat. The low rails I'm gripping with white knuckles are coming loose from rot. Cresting over the top of the fifth wave or so, we hang just an instant too long and land with a brain-rattling shudder. The captain immediately cuts the engine. All the horror stories I've heard about boats cracking and sinking in the islands come rushing back. Sure enough, a thin surge of water comes in under our butts. "*Harus kembali!*" I'm shouting to the captain, waving him back to port. His mate scurries up to the front and after a quick look at the floor just behind the bow, he too begins pointing back to the harbor. Wheeling the boat slowly downwind while more water begins to slosh in, the captain points to a funnel and bucket and tells us to bail. Gas fumes waft up from the back, where fuel residue on the outside of the tanks is now mingling with the inflow. Jeffri and I hurriedly keep up with the leak — so frantically that I accidentally chuck my bucket overboard by accident. "It's OK," the captain says, as we flatten out and speed through the harbor. His mate hands me the wad of Indonesian Rupiah I paid ten minutes ago. We bump up onto a beach and tumble out of the boat quickly, pausing only to look at a swatch of sheet metal that had been previously nailed across a crack near the bow. Now, it's clearly bent back out of place. I savor the first steps on hard ground. It's little solace for Jeffri. "I think I've lost the spirit for the trip," he says, stone-faced. Reaching the small guesthouse on the main drag of shops he adds, "I'm in shock," and promptly falls asleep for four hours; he later admits he's not as good a swimmer as he'd initially led on.

Although I envisioned us breast stroking to shore in the warm water with the aid of our lifejackets, I'm a bit shaken, too, and I distractedly scrub at my oil-stained clothes for hours. Eventually, we'll learn that three longboats had accidents today along this coast, and a fourth boat, a 12-meter cargo ship carrying a load of people, sprung a leak and threw a vegetable seller overboard while listing in big swells. (He was pulled to safety.) It's a tenuous existence for people here, where one small mistake in the face of the elements can be costly, and vigilance and good instincts are indispensable.

In the post-Aceh era, people are restlessly trying to retool those instincts for the tsunami threat, which seems to sit somewhere between the daily milieu of capsized boats, ballooned jaws, dysentery and the supernatural. In the Sipora village of Berimanua, locals were too spooked to stick around after a small tsunami there in 2007. In addition to the knee-deep flood, a muddy section of an embankment behind the village gave way in the earthquake shaking and sent a giant hardwood sliding down on top of a spring people depended on for water. Then, three waterspouts had sprung up from the ground, and a long opening in the earth formed right down the center of the housing area. A trio of elder residents suffered heart attacks from all the stress. "Some people think what happened there was a curse for what people in the world were doing," says the village's youth leader. "So, we chose a new place."

We find the village, in a former field of crops and durian trees one and a half kilometers from the old place. Berkat, as they call the new place, has a frontierish hum and hue to it, with men up in rafters banging in nails and calling out "Hallo, Mister!", children in front of the makeshift schoolhouse fashioning a bookshelf from a broken chair and scrap boards, and blackened stumps and charred logs studding the barren, muddy ground. Men in narrow dugouts filled with salvaged boards trickle in from the old, abandoned village.

The villagers here had a luxury not available to even middle-class urbanites in Padang — space. A fellow villager offered up this agricultural area to village elders after the earthquakes. Berimanuans camped out in tents for three months at the end of 2007 and on into 2008, the men sleeping mostly out in the open through the rainy season while women and children stayed undercover. (Nineteen other families from Berimanua were doing the same on the outskirts of another village across the bay, where their relatives had given them some land to resettle.) Food was incredibly scarce, and they built new shelters mainly from what they could saw from trees in the new place and what they could carry from the old. The Mentawaian district government did agree to help with the resettlement but only paid the first half of the promised $1,600 for each house in December of 2008, close to a year after villagers left the old place. Residents of the new spot earned a reputation among aid workers as an extra-hardened bunch, for both surviving a lean interim period and occasionally losing their cool with staffers from SurfAid. One aid crew filming the reconstruction efforts was shouted down by a man who told them what locals really needed was nails not more video footage.

The village head, Osmar, a small, taut 40-something farmer whose stylish O shades complete a marathoner look, pushed the community to move, and he allows that government money for new chainsaws and cement has effectively bought some catharsis in recent months. "We had three tsunamis — after Aceh, the Nias earthquake in 2005 and the 2007 earthquakes — and the people were scared," he says, walking to his emerging house, a patchwork of old whitened boards and newly cut ones at the back of the village. But, as he says, "It was devastating to knock down my old house — I had just built it two years earlier." They are still struggling to find enough food here.

And the big question is whether or not they are safer here in this new place. The new locale stayed dry during the previous tsunamis. But larger tsunamis might be an entirely different story because this new settlement is right on the beach. The little schoolhouse sits 50 meters from the water, and the escape hill that locals have identified is puny, and sits a mere five meters above sea level. Osmar gently asks if I know why this place wasn't flooded in 2007, or if there's any truth to the talk he heard of future big quakes. He's probing to see how his instincts will hold up in the long run.

Increasingly, Osmar and other Mentawaian leaders are also gauging their intuition against the science that is trickling unevenly into their community. Much of the information comes from SurfAid, a ten-year-old humanitarian group founded by a surfing doctor to stop malaria and which turned to disaster relief and then preparedness following the Aceh tsunami. With money from the Australian government, SurfAid pushed communities to identify the hazards that threatened them and then identify escape routes and other methods to lower the risk. The group capitalized on the newfound interest in earthquakes and tsunamis, including some of the fear that had been whipped up by images and rumors. "The strategy was to make them a little scared — then they'll start paying attention," says one program manager who helped run SurfAid's program and was an avid follower of Kerry Sieh's forecasts.

Running evacuation drills with villagers and teaching school kids new songs with messages about what to do during and after a quake is of real value in the communities, especially with precious few other outreach initiatives in the remote islands and nothing from the district government.

What continues to bedevil SurfAid, like Sieh and his poster-toting crew before, is how to pass along the current science of the fault to poorly educated and isolated island communities, so they'll have an accurate picture of future threats. There's an undercurrent of misinformation and some lingering suspicions of the idea of powerful earthquakes and tsunamis, even in the villages where SurfAid staff live and work.

The 'trigger' theory of earthquakes, for instance, still lives. "Some old people have a running joke: that foreigners have a remote switch and whenever there's a quake they just push a button to trigger it," a young teacher in Silabu, Sapri Was Nidar, told us. "Foreigners have reached the moon, they say, and so they have that kind of technology to bring earthquakes."

But Sapri, who said she understood quakes and tsunamis and had been working for most of the last four years to teach basic geology to her elementary students, also exposed some resentment beyond flippant conspiracy theories. "Why are people coming from another place, people who know about the instrument and how to predict things and the locals don't know anything about the tools?" she said, referring to the global positioning system unit in Silabu. "We don't have any information. They put this on our land, we protect it, keep children away but we don't know anything about it. The guys from LIPI [The Indonesian Institute of Science] just come, check the unit and leave." (Unfortunately, Natawidjaja and his crew, running on a tight schedule, did just that when they dropped us off in Silabu. In the swirl of activity in the last few years, the memory of their pre-Aceh video presentation in August 2004 has also faded in Silabu — I had to convince the village elders over many doubts that the scientists had set up a screen and projector in town.)

Stopping to look at the global positioning units used to measure the up and down motions of the islands, it became easier to appreciate the confusion. The small sticker explaining the device and telling people to leave it alone describes it as an 'earthquake and tsunami detection tool'. But, as all the scientists using the instrument know, it does not detect tsunamis. The data is for long-term forecasts. The frustrating description only causes people like Sapri to exclaim, as she did, "We want to know whether there's a tsunami and how big!" and figure that information exists and is going to someplace like California, Singapore or Jakarta and staying there.

SurfAid staffers who end up passing information along to villagers in the Mentawais breed their own inferiority complex. Villagers in Silabu said that a staff member had recently predicted an earthquake would arrive in the next 10 days. This wasn't the first time the particular guy had made a prediction, they said, and he'd been right before: after the two large 2007 quakes he told the women to stay on the hill because there might be aftershocks, which there were. He also said there'd be more big rumbles in the future, which proved correct six months later. But the village head Demas' daughter said the prediction was wrong this time and had just stirred up needless fear. "I want to tell [the SurfAider] there's been no quake and he's a liar," she said. "They don't claim to have more knowledge than us," she continued, "But he comes from SurfAid so he knows more than us."

***

To an outsider, it looks like an increasingly tall and complex task for locals to settle into a new life in the island, facing all sorts of novel trials — sniffing out junk science and hoaxes — with not much more than their own wits. But it can be done.

At the southern tip of Sipora, near the village of Katiet, we find foreign surfers catching the last of good swells, while locals over the ridgeline at another settlement are in an ongoing debate about their decision to move closer to an ascendable part of the ridge.

The new Gobik settlement is taking a makeshift shape in the

form of scrap wood shacks in a sandy clearing carved out of a coconut grove, near the base of the ridge and 100 meters from a dreamy, horseshoe-shaped white sand beach with no one on it.

But when the usual posse of men gathers that night on a house porch, we learn that seven of 20 households, including some close relatives, have stayed behind in the original village to the north. Those left behind would later tell us they didn't want to leave houses they'd only recently built, out of expensive concrete. One man said that he didn't believe in the safety of the new place, even though he was nearly surrounded by a swamp at the old spot. So he and others stayed put, next to the sledgehammered shells of houses abandoned and salvaged by moving neighbors. (The destroyed homes look eerily as if they've been bitten into by tsunami waves)

Even the strong proponents of the moving plan are having their doubts. Sitting around the porch at the new spot, Lasker, the broad-shouldered, deliberate youth leader who's been voluntarily trained by SurfAid to lead disaster preparedness in the village says, "We felt the 2007 quake very strongly and yet there was no tsunami…" Across from him, a young man blurts out triumphantly, "Yeah, now the Mentawai earthquakes don't have tsunami potential. I'm doubting it!"

Alpaus, a recent head of Gobik who had pushed hard for the move, glares at the kid, who turns out to be his son: "There is still potential." The conversation then blows up into so much chatter that we can't follow. But Alpaus' son eventually retreats. "OK, I'm still scared," he says.

Lasker produces an article from SurfAid's monthly newspaper, about a recently mapped underwater seamount to the south of the islands that could be a volcano storing up a tsunami-generating explosion. People have been talking about it repeatedly this week throughout the islands. We don't know that Indonesian scientists in Jakarta and Padang already doubt the volcano is active and within a month the national technology agency will say it's not. Alpaus, the 50-year-old former headman, says right then and there in Gobik, "This is like Ripley's Believe It or Not."

"I'm afraid of all the research that comes out, but I see the point of it so I take in all the information," he continues, a smile spreading across his face. "In the Bible, it says that there will be earthquakes everywhere. It's the sign of the end of the world. I'm not sure which chapter it's in but it's there. And so the pastors have been saying we should ask for forgiveness. People have different reactions. Some feel helpless. Some say don't give up. And so when SurfAid says we should run to the hill after a quake, some people just stay in the lowlands."

The new beachside settlement of Gobik carved from a coconut plantation. (Photo by Jeffri Adriyanto)

Alpaus has stressed the safety of the new place, closer to the hill. But he has this cheeky smirk when he talks about earthquakes, to go with his pointed face and small, wiry frame that he wraps around itself when he's sitting, so he looks like a grinning upright gecko. (His favorite shirt on the days we visit is a black and yellow golf shirt with the words 'FIT N FRESH' over the left breast.) When the old Mentawaian myths about earthquakes come up in conversation, he says, "The quakes used to mean fruit harvest, now they mean soul harvest." And about the people left behind in the old settlement, he adds, "They're just saying 'Let us die here'."

He's droll because he can filter what he's hearing. The guidelines now are: believe nothing religiously but note everything carefully.

He has knocked some of the manic nature out of this earthquake-shaken moment by building a sense of the islands' dynamic geologic past. He's heard about an Australian scientist who'd discovered corals up on the ridgeline about four hours north of here. He's absorbed the story of past great earthquakes and tsunamis in the area, from videos that SurfAid has shown in Gobik. "They say this area has seen past quakes, in a time when the ocean was closer to the hills here," Alpaus says. "We know they found corals in the hills up the coast. And we know that the ocean used to be here, where we are today, in the past. People lived up on the hills."

And with some cool perspective he and other leaders in town have looked over today's threat and decided they should land here, in a friend's coconut grove at the base of the hill.

"Maybe God wants to make this ocean again," Alpaus says, and they'll need to go high. But for now he and other leaders have decided to keep one foot in both places.

On our last morning in Gobik, after a mouth-watering bowl

High above Gobik, an emergency post takes shape. (Photo by Jeffri Adriyanto)

of Lasker's wife's sticky coconut rice, we head with him for the ridge behind the new settlement with Lasker. Each of us hauls two planks each and trails him up the steep, packed-mud path; he scampers barefoot and with his machete in his off hand, steady as a mountain goat. In a minute or two, we're looking from inside a new wooden house frame over the tops of the coconut plantation to a sliver of aqua ocean. SurfAid has offered $3,200 for materials for the establishment of this emergency post and others like it around the islands. It will have enough room for the women and children to sleep, and a small room with kitchen utensils and food stores. They're using cement footings and metal braces holding the studs to the footings, in the hopes the *posko* survives a great earthquake. They'll also build a latrine and plant a few crops outside the house.

The theory is they could ride out any disaster's aftermath here.

Today, Lasker would like to finish the roof. One man is already up in the rafters, measuring for cross beams and over the next 45 minutes or so, another six guys trek up the hill and join in. Gulton, who lent us a room in his house, pounds in floorboards to a set beat — *ratiTAT ratiTAT ratiTAT TAT TAT TAT*. Alpaus shaves the edges down on planks, while his son fiddles with the radio, trying to pick up one of two mainland stations. Lasker marks some boards with string dipped in engine oil. This is all going up with a heavy dose of elbow grease, which the group has committed to put in for free, two days a week for this month and next. It's a new twist on the sort of purposeful longhouse raising that is age-old, and that colors the old Mentawai stories and taboos of earthquakes. And in this scene at Gobik, these parables don't seem lost but merely re-imagined.

9.

What's a Warning System For?

In the glassed-in, two-story mission control room of north Jakarta's new national earthquake and tsunami early warning center, a loud, electronic bell clangs like a door chime. Atop one row of computers, a white police light begins to whir and a mechanized voice drones over the loudspeakers, "Earthquake, Magnitude 3.7 at 10:58, requires peaking". Bayu Pranata, a 28-year-old seismologist in a powder-blue uniform shirt and navy pants, hustles to his computer station, as a bull's eye marking a tentative epicenter appears near the island of Sulawesi on the soaring digital map of Indonesia on the front wall. Pranata pores over the peaks and valleys of several seismographs on his screen, registering from stations around the country. He finds the initial peak of the quake — the blast of energy known as the 'P-wave' — and marks it with his cursor on each graph. With the arrival times of this first pulse, and the second known as the 'S-wave', the computer, with a little guidance from Bayu, updates the location of the earthquake within two minutes. The computer also crunches an initial magnitude from the earthquake readings sent in from field stations.

A button image at the bottom of Bayu's screen reads 'Send This Data'. If the earthquake had topped 7 in magnitude and occurred shallower than 70 kilometers undersea, he would consider it a tsunami threat and could pass the location and size on to the desk directly behind him. From there, another seismologist on his seven-member team would pipe a 'tsunami potential' bulletin out to cell phone companies, TV stations and local governments in affected areas. The information on the tiny Sulawesi earthquake this morning comes to the point of reaching public channels with very little fuss from Bayu, talking as he clicks away on the computer as if he is texting a friend.

Although the warning system will be of little help to off-the-grid Mentawai islanders, Padang's chances of getting quick information from Jakarta are certainly better than the day of the disastrous Aceh quake, when readings bigger than anybody had ever dreamed of hit antiquated seismometers, and it took the Jakarta team five hours to get the size and the location of the quake right. The Jakarta warning center is proving every day that the message that reached Padang Mayor Fauzi Bahar a mere five minutes after the first earthquake in September 2007 was no fluke.

But effective warnings are about more than people in Jakarta locating an earthquake, knowing its correct size and sending that info out through the airwaves. It's becoming clear that in this sprawling system built with 45 million Euros worth of help from the German government, speed isn't the biggest challenge.

"It turns out monitoring and dissemination of the information has been relatively easy — we've reached our goal of getting it out [from headquarters] under five minutes in four years," says Fauzi, who oversees the earthquake and tsunami warning system in Jakarta.

The problem is on the back end. Five years after the Aceh tragedy, in mid-2009, neither officials in Jakarta nor in Padang have resolved who should get the information, what they hear and how they hear it, and other cities are not much farther along. It's as if a car company had finished an extremely powerful, cutting edge engine before it had any idea what sort of car the engine would drive.

Meanwhile people on the street in Padang have heard about the system, and are beginning to see it as a first line of defense.

Once when I challenged a couple of high school grads in the city to tell me whether they were scared of a tsunami, they were flippant at first — "I'm preparing a surfboard for the event!" — before pronouncing an overriding faith in the government and the new system.

"There's an alarm not far from here, near my house, and if there's a quake with the potential for a tsunami it'll go off and people are expected to move," said one guy, referring to Padang's sole alarm that can be triggered by the Jakarta warning center. "We believe it will work and it will prevent casualties."

"People are trained now to listen to the government," said another dude. "They'll turn on the radio and wait for the alarm."

Then a university student and community worker said, "I just believe in it because I'm not a scientist. Let's leave it to the scientists to build."

But unless something changes, the hi-tech messages from Jakarta will dissolve in confusion in those frantic minutes after a big quake in a coastal city. That's if the message ever gets through to a place likely suffering from wide scale power outages. The worth of this much heralded — and very expensive — technology is up for grabs.

***

Fauzi is a shy, bespectacled 55-year-old, with a PhD from Rensselaer Polytechnic Institute, in the U.S. state of New York, and he seems to be quietly and politely holding back overwhelmed-ness. In his spacious but sparse office down the hall from the warning center control room, boxes are piled up for yet another move — the geophysical and meteorology agency has expanded twice in the last five years and has even added a third leg to its stool: climatology. Fauzi's wooden wall clock bears a growing pile of more than three dozen name badges hung by their lanyards, from the endless international meetings on early warning systems and disaster preparedness since the 2004 tsunami. As he talks, he closes his eyes every now and then with what looks like exasperation until I realize he's searching his crowded brain for answers and their English equivalent.

In August of 2003, Fauzi (who uses only his highly common first name and isn't related to the mayor of Padang) and his colleagues met with American, Japanese and Russian counterparts at a conference in West Java to mark the 120th anniversary of the eruption of Krakatau and the deadly accompanying tsunami. The memories were still fresh from a 1992 tsunami that had killed over

2,000 people on Flores Island in eastern Indonesia, and the deadly 1998 waves in neighboring Papua New Guinea. Several presenters pressed for a tsunami warning system in the country, including some local leaders in coastal provinces.

The next year, Fauzi says he drew up a rough plan for the system. "We had in mind a program that would target support from the international community," he says. They also planned to lobby local government and the national legislature in the hopes of moving the system up on the national priority list. But that was as far they got. When the tsunami hit Aceh and elsewhere, Fauzi says he beat back the tears and thought, *It's too soon.*

Prior to that moment, tsunami-warning systems were primarily Japanese and American ventures. The United States began its system after a 1946 Aleutian Islands earthquake flooded Hawaii; Japanese seismologists started tracking earthquakes with tsunami potential in the 1950s. The push to modernize and link both systems followed the 1960 magnitude 9.5 Chilean quake, which was the biggest ever recorded and sent tsunamis clear across the Pacific that killed several dozen people in Hilo, Hawaii and 120 people some 16,000 kilometers away in Japan.

These long distance tsunamis, so deadly in 2004 as well, prove especially challenging because people don't get that early warning sign of a powerful earthquake before the tsunamis arrive. Warning systems can be invaluable aides for an unassuming public (although there is accompanying ocean movement to tip them off). So since the 1960s, the Americans' Pacific Tsunami Warning Center near Honolulu has been the UN-anointed tsunami watcher for the entire Pacific. It now keeps a close eye on underwater earthquakes using a network of global seismic

GLOBAL WAVE

This series of time-elapse images from the 2004 tsunami originating near Sumatra shows how the wave crests (grey) distribute outward in a matter of hours, finally reaching the far extent of the globe. (Credited to NCTE — NOAA Center for Tsunami Research)

Hours since event: 00:00

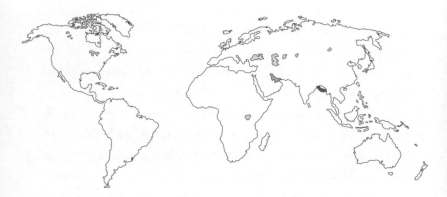

Hours since event: 03:00

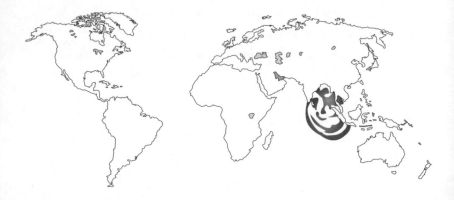

Hours since event: 10:00

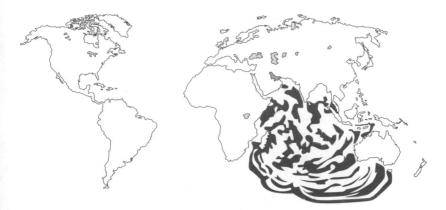

Hours since event: 33:30

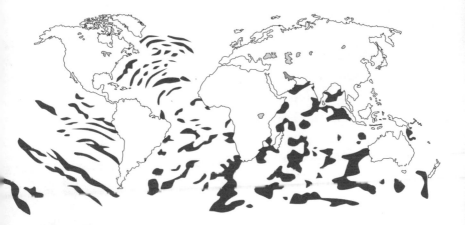

monitors, including, lately, those operated by Nuclear Test-Ban Treaty Organization to detect underground nuclear tests. Once the quake registers, the center tracks the progression of tsunami waves moving the water column across the Pacific, using pressure gauges scattered along the ocean's bottom and satellite-linked, through surface buoys, to Hawaii. The developing situation, over hours, is critical information for potential victims far afield — the 1960 tsunami reached Hilo, Hawaii in 15 hours and the Japanese island of Honshu in 22.

The Hawaii and Tokyo centers knew the rough parameters of a threatening quake of at least magnitude 8 quake off Aceh within 15 to 30 minutes of the event in 2004, but they didn't have contacts at most disaster offices around the Indian Ocean. As a result, countries like India, Sri Lanka and Thailand remained in the dark outside the heavy shaking zone. The 2004 tsunami has provided a watershed moment similar to the 1960s' in warning systems funding and interest, both of which had slowed to a trickle, outside Japan. For one thing, the Hawaii and Tokyo centers now have the phone numbers for disaster headquarters in 26 of 28 Indian Ocean countries. And the UN has charged them with sending out far-field warnings in the Indian Ocean, until regional countries can take over in 2011.

With the impressive offer of the German government, however, Japanese and American scientific teams contributed only a few instruments and were left on the sidelines of a new Indonesian system with ambitious plans.

The goal of Fauzi's team and their German partners, led by the Potsdam-based Geophysical Research Center, is to rapidly increase the earthquake info coming into Jakarta, and the ability to crunch it in accurate models to determine how severe tsunami waves are before they hit shore. The group has flooded Sumatra, Java, and to a lesser extent, the outlying islands with modern seismometers, increasing the count from 34 to 180. To build models of what a tsunami will look like in key vulnerable cities, German scientists trekked out on an exhaustive mapping exercise, using satellite images, the Space Shuttle mapping data, low-altitude flyovers in airplanes toting high-resolution cameras, and depth-sounding boats. Global Positioning System stations deployed through the archipelago will measure land uplifts and depressions in real-time after a quake. The team hopes that enough of that data can quickly show how the sea-bottom has deformed. That picture will then be matched with tsunami models drawn from over 2,500 different scenarios, and in theory, allow warning center staff to issue tsunami bulletins targeted at specific areas. Finally, gauges in the open-ocean and in harbors will attempt to confirm what's actually happening in the sea. Like colleagues elsewhere, the German group is trying to make tsunami prediction as accurate as meteorology. "When scientists tried to do weather prediction 50 years ago, people thought they were nuts," says Jorn Behrens, who led the design of the warning system's tsunami model. "When we propose this, we are called nuts. But in an industrialized era, this is the way we need to go to save lives and property."

"This is state of the art," Behrens says of the tsunami model, which built on expertise German scientists developed modeling storm surges off their menacing North Sea coast. The tsunami simulations on land are accurate to about 50 meters, or one city block, which was applicable for city planning purposes. "You could say 'OK, we need to put a hospital out of this area' and just account for the margin of error of the model," he says. Already, a compilation of his group's tsunami scenarios are being used by the government of Denpasar, in Bali, to determine high risk areas of the city. Cilacap in Java is also using the German tsunami maps.

Other scientists in the international tsunami community have plenty of doubts about the accuracy of the German-built model, however. The way tsunami waves move through the ocean and then interact with the land is incredibly complex, and a tsunami model is like a fine wine — it gets better with age, as modelers add some complexities and shed others and inch it ever closer to reality. German scientists early in the real life trials of the system are 'reinventing the wheel', as one non-German modeler put it. They're also feeding in data from earthquakes off Java that are poorly understood. Many of the instruments are also not functioning; nearly half of the two dozen ocean pressure gauges off Indonesia were not working correctly at the end of 2009. And the models have yet to narrow warnings to anything more specific than 'tsunami potential'.

***

Fauzi admits this is eroding the urgency of the warnings. Between 2007 and 2009, the agency sent out 21 'tsunami potential' messages, but the earthquakes only produced five tsunamis that registered on any ocean gauges. Only one did any significant damage. The other four were technically tsunami but so small that before gauges were set in the ocean, these waves wouldn't have really existed. So Fauzi has had to decide if the warning center staff should squelch the news that these small tsunamis are out there, to head off unnecessary panic, or be open about the processes that they're now observing.

The agency's stance as of late 2009 is to cancel any warning if a tsunami turns out to be less than 50 centimeters. For warnings that stand, the center is hoping to refine the warning to Red, which would mean a tsunami potentially over five meters, or Orange, meaning one between five meters and 50 centimeters. Fauzi imagines people at the beach and coastal neighborhoods knowing that after a Red warning, they need to find high ground quickly, and after an Orange they would at least back away from the coast. "Everybody is asking how big this potential is," he says. "And that's why we need the scenarios."

But Fauzi and his colleagues in Jakarta wash their hands off making sure the right citizens on the ground actually receive and respond to the warnings. His agency has scattered a few sirens around Sumatra, which can be triggered by the Jakarta warning center. But their job is only to see that local decision makers like the mayor or district head get the bulletin. Beyond that, under Indonesian law, "Response belongs to the local government," Fauzi says firmly. But without the best minds in the country focused on delivering the message from the top right down to neighborhoods like those along the beach in Padang, city leaders are, in 2009, struggling mightily with how to get a warning out clearly.

City officials have been hung up for years trying to figure out how big an area is really at risk in a tsunami of five or six meters because the Padang area is now a scientific hotspot. Between Sieh's group, Behrens', and other German groups and Indonesian scientists, there's a bumper crop of risk maps that have circulated in recent years. Sieh and Natawidjaja contend that the city should prepare for the worst possible tsunami based on historic examples, while Behrens' group is eager to use a compilation of its myriad scenarios of different tsunamis large and small.

At a conference in Padang in mid-2008, scientists from Sieh's group and the German coalition agreed to share data and create a new risk map. But with little prodding from public servants, they took another eight months to figure out how to swap the data and begin working on the new scenarios, and by mid-2009 it is still not done.

"We need this kind of map; a science-based recommendation," says Harald Spahn from the German agency for technical cooperation, who has been working with local Indonesian governments trying to use the warning system. "The Padang government has said they cannot make decisions. So they need options based on the latest knowledge. I say let's put everyone's logos on there and get on with it. There are thousands of lives we're dealing with here. If we use the wrong approach, we can do a lot of harm."

Meanwhile, a broadcast system for warnings is slipping through the cracks. Aim Zein, the radio station owner, has been unable to get anybody in City Hall excited about the subject. The current de-facto method in mid-2009 of telling people about a tsunami: hoping the power is on, so people can get a message from the mayor, relayed from Jakarta, on the public Radio Republik Indonesia station. If the power's out, those sophisticated warnings from Jakarta — the ones that tell people where to evacuate from and how big the tsunami might be — will be totally lost.

This would be more maddening if it weren't so common. Getting warnings to people and getting them to respond is tough all over, whether you're in Hawaii or Thailand.

Thailand lost over 8,000 people in the 2004 tsunami, a third of them foreign tourists. Visitor revenues, typically about 6% of the Thai economy, were down by more than two-thirds the next year. In the rush to project safety to foreigners, the Thai government embraced warning towers that can broadcast a short message in five languages. Aid agencies suggested cheaper methods that might tap into things people were already using, like TVs, radios, cell phones (Thailand is not subject to the same earthquake driven power outages as Padang, because they're further from the fault line). But the government went with towers, in no small measure because they're also visible totems of a prepared country.

The towers have had plenty of problems. Some villages in the vulnerable Krabi Province, the most popular among island-flocking tourists, are out of range of the tower speakers. In other bustling market areas, it's difficult to hear the announcements over the din of motorbikes, restaurants and the other mundane sounds of Thai life. Dozens of the towers either aren't linked into the national warning center in Bangkok or don't function at all. Others have been prone to false alarms. At least one village in the Krabi area disconnected its loudspeaker after it malfunctioned and was stuck in alarm mode. The Thai system also failed to give out any instructions after the September 2007 earthquakes in Sumatra, leaving people to fend for themselves. There was no actual tsunami threat but international reports about the tsunami on TV drove people to high ground needlessly.

Aceh, which received several new sirens from Jakarta after the tsunami, has also battled malfunction. After the faulty wiring triggered alarms in June 2007, sending Banda Aceh into a traffic-jammed, emotional wreck, one group of villagers threw rocks at its alarm until it broke.

Places with working broadcast systems face their own set of problems. One of the reasons people died in Hilo, Hawaii, in 1960 was because they'd lost faith in the system of sirens established on the coast there in the 1950s, which had repeatedly delivered alarms for tsunamis that never came or that people didn't notice. The sirens blared again around 8.30 pm in the evening in May 1960, as tsunami waves streaked north from Chile. Sure enough, the first low wave hit without much punch just after midnight. Warning-weary folks then returned to the shore neighborhoods, assured by at least one police officer this was another minor event. But after 1 am, a four-meter wall of water slammed into Hilo and caught much of the city off guard, killing 61 people.

In parts of Thailand, Sri Lanka and now in Padang, the local people's answer to distrusted or half-baked national systems is to take on the responsibility of warning themselves.

Radio station owner Aim Zein, who's no longer working on the official warning system, is taking the initiative to spread the word from Jakarta on his own, using BlackBerry groups with dozens of phone numbers and email addresses in them. When Jakarta sends out an earthquake or tsunami bulletin, which individuals can sign up to receive, Zein forwards it around the city with a few touches on the hand-held device. He's also lobbying the geophysical and meteorological agency to put a satellite on his roof that would link his radio station directly to the warning system in Jakarta. He can run his station on generators in a pinch, and would broadcast the warnings himself. "Why not, it's not against the law?" he says, in his usual brassy radio voice. "We always make the mistake of thinking that we have to go up the chain of command, from local, provincial, then national. Why not just bypass? It's a public warning we're talking about, man. Go direct!" Meanwhile, he's formed a partnership with a German company that would like to get Padang to use a modified radio — which could deliver text and voice commands on a dedicated FM band — right into people's homes. Zein would stand to make some money if that deal did go through, but he's open about it: he'd be quite happy to be called a tsunami communications entrepreneur.

Over at the West Sumatra disaster management office, set up as part of a national initiative after the Aceh tsunami, staffers are now bucking the idea of waiting for messages from Jakarta and have cobbled together their own parallel tsunami recognition system. The group has placed a water level gauge north of the city in the town of Pariaman, a closed circuit TV camera watching the shore from a beachside hotel and a local accelerometer to measure ground shaking. When an earthquake hits, staff members in their own small mission control room lined with TV monitors check public internet sites run by the U.S. Geological Survey, the Hawaii tsunami warning center and the German geophysical agency, as well as Jakarta's warning center, to look at the size and location of the earthquake. If the main power grid and telecommunication lines go down, they can run off backup power systems and use a satellite internet connection to get the info they need. From the local camera shots on the shore and the earthquake size and location, they can make recommendations to the local government about tsunami potentials. Regardless of how an earthquake has wrecked national communications, they can circulate a definitive yes or no about a tsunami coming from within the community, on a special VHF radio band that they've trained the local media to monitor.

"Here we thought of scenarios, and then we built the system," says Ade Edward, an old university pal of Danny Natawidjaja's who heads the disaster management office. "With the national system, they just built it first. Systems could be bottom up or top down but it has to be based on the real situation. Each area is different, and technology needs to be applied in a proper way. We use cheap stuff."

Redundancy is good, but parallel systems have the power to confuse. What if the local group and Jakarta manage to get conflicting messages about an approaching tsunami to the mayor? Ade's not worried; he's pretty sure his group will react first, what with lines to Jakarta likely to be dead. "One thing's for certain, the power *will* be off," he says.

The potential confusion, like all of the warning system's struggles, points to the importance of people learning to interpret tsunami risks for themselves. In Padang and every other place close to tsunami-generating faults, that information is free and immediately available — in the natural warning signs — if you know how to read them.[*] Even people supporting the construction of the Indonesian system are beginning to see this. "People are now understanding what a system can and can't do," says Harald Spahn, the German consultant to local Indonesian governments. "I think the result is you should not rely on the early warning system only.

---

[*] *Rarely, a tsunami-generating earthquake will not be felt by cities nearby. This happened in Nicaragua in 1992, when a tsunami arrived in the middle of the night and caught people sleeping. Still, tide gauges or a harbor patrol can observe strange sea recession.*

You should rely on the natural warning signs [an extremely strong earthquake, broken buildings and the ocean receding] from the earthquake and then make use of the warning system to quickly confirm whether there's actually a tsunami or not."

But it's a shame that the workers with the German-Indonesian warning system didn't realize how useful those first warnings were four years previous, before the lion's share of the 45 million Euros project budget was committed to gadgets whose message is still struggling to be heard.

10.
The Rising

Jeffri Adriyanto was supposed to be on the second floor of his college in central Padang, in the first meeting of Literary Research Methods at the start of a new term, at around 5 pm on September 30, 2009. Instead, he blew off the first session, figuring it would be slow. He took a nap at home that afternoon. Then, just after 5 pm, he decided to go work out at the gym where he's a personal trainer, in Pondok, the oldest section of Padang, near the Arau River. But as he rode out onto the small lane behind his house, across the river from Pondok, his motorcycle suddenly ground to a halt, as if somebody was pushing against the front wheel. Very quickly, people began pouring out of their houses and into the street, screaming, even crying. A wavy, disorienting sensation turned to quick, head-rattling jolts. A cement wall collapsed onto the lane, narrowly missing Jeffri. He stayed on his vintage motorbike with its clanking exhaust, and circled slowly back to his house. His grandmother and his mother, who'd come scrambling down from the second floor, steadied themselves in the front yard. There, they rode out the last low rumbles of the one-minute shake together. When it was done, they searched the boxy, concrete house and found it had survived with only cracks in the plaster.

Still, the quake had been unmistakably strong and jarring. The neighbors, recovering from the shock of the shake, streaked down the lane and toward the flanks of nearby Gunung Padang. "The water is rising! The water is rising!" Adriyanto heard people saying, with an eye on the river. He couldn't see if that was true, but erring on the side of caution, he told his mother and grandmother to follow the neighbors uphill. They wouldn't budge. The phones were dead and they hadn't heard from his older sister, who was still at work in the business district.

Around 15 minutes later, she rolled up on her bike. Many of the three and four-story bank buildings that lined her route home had been crippled into ruins. The Mayor's office building she'd passed was standing, but sliced as if with a sharp knife, and the open air market behind it was emitting thick black smoke. Imelda said another building had also crumpled: the three-story Apotek Sari, the pharmacy where Adriyanto's friends Ivonne Linardi and Johnson Chandra lived and worked. At their peak business hour of 5 pm, they were almost certainly inside. The previous July, Adriyanto spent two weeks talking about nothing but tsunamis with me in the Mentawai Islands and he knew the risk to Padang well. But in that lull after the earthquake, his buddies called. He jumped on his motorbike and sped across the Arau on a nearby bridge, and into the aging heart of Pondok — Chinatown — where the tsunami of 1797 had deposited that giant English ship.

The rest of the city, too, was conflicted. Authorities were going incommunicado as huge sections of the place lost electricity to toppled power poles. The largest cell phone network, run by the state-owned Telkomsel, dropped out of service, and several of the radio stations went offline because of the power outages and damaged equipment. Nobody on the street was hearing much of anything from Jakarta or its emissaries, neither on the radio nor through text messages. But the earthquake seemed to be surely a magnitude 8, and possibly even a 9 — only one that big could cause the pavement to wave up and down like a rug, as one observer put it. Certainly a tsunami would follow.

In the silence, people decided for themselves what to do. Some jettisoned for high ground. Patra Dewi, the organizer, headed toward Gunung Pangilun, the small hill near her house in the family car — she hit a massive traffic jam a half a kilometer before the hill. Other routes to high ground were similarly jamming up all over the city. But the city was also gridlocked because other people were crossing town to gather up their families, and a third class did something curious: they went *towards* the water. Not sure if a tsunami was on its way, they wanted to be sure before they ran. The beach began to fill with eager watchers. In one sense it's promising: they'd learned that a receding tide was a telltale sign. But it could have proved deadly, because there's no way all of the people — witnesses described a cast of thousands down on the coast — could have made it to safety in time, not least the elderly folks from Chinatown who said they followed the crowds down to the beach.

Meanwhile, emergency workers around town improvised quickly to get confirmation of a tsunami. Staff in two disaster management offices, the city's as well as the province's, repaired their internet connections and downloaded internet messages coming from the warning center in Jakarta. The word was the earthquake had only been a magnitude 7.5 and too deep to generate a dangerous tsunami (a 0.2-meter wave did result). Officials began passing the message along on radio bands typically used by search and rescue workers and other emergency workers on their walkie-talkies. But it was another 30 minutes at least before Mayor Fauzi got the word out on FM through a repaired state radio station. And few actually heard it, what with the traffic chaos and power outages. Red Cross workers made do: when the message came through walkie-talkies, they took to spreading it around their office at a major intersection in downtown using megaphones. In a seaside neighborhood where Kogami had trained and equipped volunteers with their own emergency radios, the volunteers spread the message simply by walking around and telling neighbors.

In the din, determined, unsure folks ditched their cars and soldiered on uphill or safely across the Banda Bakali River to an inland ring road that people consider the mark of safety. Some took two and three hours to get there on foot. Others climbed in whatever they could: one guy told me he jumped into the back of an empty ambulance with his family.

Jeffri Adriyanto zipped against traffic and found his friend Ivonne's father waiting in front of the pharmacy, where the third floor had collapsed through the second and come to rest over the red sign that once welcomed customers in.

Ivonne's father's phone rang, despite all the dead or busy signals other people were getting. It was a friend of the trapped couple, calling from Jakarta; she'd just received a change-in-status from Johnson's BlackBerry reading, "Help us." Ivonne's father stepped into a narrow slot in the ruins and began pulling at the rubble, but a few minutes later he returned with one of his hands sliced and bleeding. Jeffri and Imelda went across the street and explained their situation to a military officer at the base there, asking him to help or to call the local search and rescue chapter, but the officer shrugged saying there was nothing he could do. When Jeffri climbed up on top of the rubble he couldn't find a way in either. Finally, they bashed a lock on a gate to the side of the building and made their way into a back alley, and there, Jeffri spied a small hole in the pile. He crawled in and saw a metal door he recognized from the old pharmacy, and he called out. Johnson answered, "I'm not far from the door!"

With small hammers, Jeffri pounded away at some of the fallen concrete, and painstakingly pushed through to Johnson's spot. He was wedged into a tiny space formed by a heavy wooden cabinet that had fallen on a plastic computer desk and was holding up debris that had rained down from above. They decided to wait for an electric saw to pry him out, and went instead to help Ivonne, who was making faint sounds from the other side of the space. Adriyanto followed her cries with a flashlight and found Ivonne close to the rear of the rubble, about chest high on an intact section of the stairs she'd been running down when the second floor came down on top of her.

To get to her, Jeffri bent down on all fours and tunneled under a stretch of wall balanced precariously on a refrigerator tipped on its side. He and Ivonne's uncle used their hands and the backs of hammers to chip at the concrete; Jeffri's hands and shins began to scratch and bleed because he was still in his workout shorts. The contents of Johnson and Ivonne's third floor apartment were splayed around them: luggage, a picture frame, a second fridge that the two workers raided for Heinekens at one point. A couple of times the remaining roof shook, raining dust and rubble down through the ruins — either from aftershocks or people walking up on top, Jeffri couldn't be sure. "Tell them to stop!" Ivonne yelled. As Jeffri worked himself under the wall section, people outside, including his sister, watched nervously through the gaps in the rubble, worried that an aftershock might pry the wall loose. When he finally got to Ivonne, she was bleeding from deep cuts around her right knee, and her lower back was strained so badly that Jeffri and her uncle had to carry her out.

Working with a newfound saw, they then cut through the bookshelf trapping Johnson. He emerged without a scratch.

It was now approaching 2 am. Ivonne and Johnson headed off to her family's house. Jeffri walked out into a Pondok barely scrutable for the dark and its changed form. Fires had just started as they were scrambling to get into the pharmacy. Now, the old wooden porn theater down the street was just a pile of smoldering ashes. Two blocks away, a wide street that cuts through the heart of Pondok had piled so high with brick and rubble that it was impassable. A car dealership on the corner had survived, but lost all of its upstairs bay windows and its fence of white sun blinds fluttered out into the open. He could see into second-story bedrooms, ripped open to the air. The new home of the Batang Arau café, the surfer hangout on a busy street in Pondok, had been flattened as the building next door toppled over onto it. Ambulances wailed throughout downtown, and people hustled by on foot and motorbikes; he couldn't tell whether they were driven by worry or just excited to see the city turned upside down, now that the initial shock of the quake had worn off.

After the earthquake, the pharmacy Apotek Sari and neighboring shophouses form a heap. (Photo by Paramesh Banerjee)

A huge crowd had gathered outside the Ambacang Hotel, where rescue teams with excavators were trying to get into the six-story block of rooms at the back that had caved in, and a restaurant and conference area that had pancaked — the latter in the midst of a training session for dozens of Prudential Insurance staff. At a shophouse a few streets away, a friend's mother was trapped alive and people were trying to get her oxygen to calm her respiratory condition.

He eventually motored over to his college and found it a mess. Shaped like a pair of tall file cabinets, one had collapsed completely and the other had lost the lower two levels of drawers. A stairwell on the right side had crumpled, and alumni and families of students paced around the rubble; all of his classmates on the second floor had run out of the building before it collapsed, but people from the third floor had not. There was no rescue equipment yet and people were growing more frantic by the minute.

***

Centered just 60 kilometers to the north of Padang, the earthquake's shock waves came quick and furiously at the city.

This caused buildings to sway back and forth like boats, the mass of the structure drifting outside its foundation. Only a well-built structure, with walls and columns thickened to hold more of a load than they do on an ordinary day, will stand up to an earthquake like that on September 30. Indonesia has had strong laws about earthquake engineering on the books since the mid-1980s, but enforcement is so weak and construction methods are so wildly divergent that even some government buildings and the most modern, sought-after spaces weren't equipped to stand up to a moderate earthquake. The Ambacang Hotel, popular among business travelers and foreign tourists, had added the six floors of rooms to the back of a turn-of-the-century Dutch shophouse in 2006, but the columns builders had used were far too narrow to hold the addition in the quake.

What's more, many of the buildings that had once been identified as escape towers, because they were tall and in low-lying areas, were now diminished heaps of concrete and steel: the Ambacang Hotel, Jeffri's college, a second language school, one of the main banks. Other escape designates were only partially standing, including two of the main hospitals. On the central north-south thoroughfare lined with multi-story government offices, one after another of the older buildings had dropped to their knees. Many built in the last decade or two were still upright, but their windows had blown out or deep gashes were carved into their walls. Just about the only modern building that survived without serious damage was owned by the cellular provider, Telkomsel. A sturdy, colorful fortress built to the latest earthquake standards, it had an exterior stairwell that people on the ground could easily climb to escape a potential tsunami. But when neighborhood residents tried to use the stairwell, they found it locked.

The post-mortem is already shaping up among relief workers from at least 70 international agencies, diplomats, journalists and scientists at the governor's mansion, where helicopters are using the front lawn as a landing pad and search and rescue teams from Singapore and Australia are camped out with their dogs in tent cities when I arrive 36 hours after the quake. I get one of the last rooms at the usually quiet Hotel Padang down the street, where single-story room blocks and thick walls have left it as one of two functional hotels and piling up with visitors and wealthy Padangans, also searching for answers.

"There are just so many textbook cases out there where the buildings weren't constructed to withstand the load and the first floor collapsed," Paramesh Banerjee, a geophysicist from the Earth Observatory of Singapore, explains to one resident; Banerjee already has a slew of pictures to prove it. I also run into Sieh, who has been traveling with an Australian TV crew. At one point, they allotted him camera time to tell the cyclical story of the Mentawai patch and confirm that the plates were still stuck together under the islands and awaiting the big slip.

I tell Sieh that the lack of tsunami this time might cast further doubt on his forecasts for Padang, since this had been such a long and strong earthquake, of the sort Patra and Kogami always told people would generate a wave train. Either he's wrong or God has spared the city, the thinking might go.

"I'm going to win that argument eventually, unless God strikes me dead first!" he says.

In the remove of the hotel and governor's mansion, it's also clear that unless someone in the city government develops some urgency about education, the people will remain utterly confused. The alertness to tsunamis is sharpening, no doubt because of grassroots efforts to build awareness. But there's a limit to what the citizen groups can do. Kogami's education has also been patchy, leaving out Chinese populations in Pondok, for instance. And there are still too many questions unanswered for the public in this maze of a place. Should we look at the water or not? Should we wait for word from the government or not, before evacuating? Nobody has stepped up to answer, five years and a half-dozen trial runs later.

"If people don't want to listen to us, what to do?" Patra Dewi says, sounding defeated. "The government has to be active. They have access to so much media every day."

***

Out in the city streets, things feel alienating and defy proper reason, especially when you haven't felt the shaking. The destruction, in a place you've once walked, eaten, and daydreamed, binds up your mind. It looks willful, too much, a giant gone insane. The list of doomed places I'd once visited or even slept in continue to mount.

The third floor of a homestay I used twice, toppled over into the neighbor's yard. The Dipo, the only hotel that would change Singapore dollars for Rupiah: finished. The city library: flattened. And a mall building on the central plaza where Kerry Sieh and I once munched on fried chicken: gutted, its interior walls and floors shredded by the shaking.

And there's a whole new round of near-miss stories as people check in through erratic surges of text messages and chance meetings at the aid staging area around the provincial governor's mansion. A student I once interviewed left his house near Gunung Pangilun for the university less than an hour before the quake hit and a brick wall collapsed into his bedroom, where he'd been resting earlier. Patra Dewi's sister was alone at their seaside house with her two young kids, when the earthquake bent the front door of the house on its hinges and trapped her inside briefly. Luckily, their home held up and no tsunami came. A pregnant expat friend who left her third floor apartment atop a shophouse at the edge of Pondok, the day before the quake: the place was totaled.

Then there are the two SurfAid volunteers we'd met in the Mentawais the previous July, the couple Matt Hannon and Stacey Howe. They were scheduled to stay in the Ambacang Hotel on the evening of the earthquake, along with another colleague, David Lange. As it turned out, Hannon's ferry from Siberut — due in on the morning of the quake — didn't leave until a day later. So instead of being upstairs with him ordering room service, Howe happened to be down in the first floor lobby when the quake struck. She ran out of the hotel into the street and turned around to see Lange hustling out from the first floor restaurant with only a handful of other guests. Then they watched the patchwork building gyrate and throw up a huge cloud of dust as it collapsed.

One person has not responded to my messages though. Nafitri Darmali was one of my first translators who gamely bounced through different neighborhoods in Padang with only a hint of what I was doing. She is also a student, with her friend Jeffri Adriyanto, at the collapsed foreign language college, STBA Prayoga. She was finishing up her senior thesis, with little course work that might bring her to the college. But on Saturday morning, two-and-a-half days after the quake, I decide to head over to the college, a short ride from the hotel, just to be sure.

A small group mills at the top of the alley that leads back to the college building. They're gathered around a fatigued soldier manning a desk with a salvaged piece of dry erase board propped up on it. All of the air drains out of my lungs when I realize this is the victims' board, with names scrawled in marker ink. I scan the list — foreign names, jumbles of letters, loopy cursive — trying to make sense of it. Nothing is connecting. I'm not reading it. *Focus. Is there an N? Yes. Nova. That's not her. Wait. No, not her.* The blood rushes back into my head.

The soldier explains that these are the 14 victims still believed to be inside. Looking up to see an excavator rolling towards the wrecked building, I follow it. In the back, the crowd comprises skinny students and pale-faced teachers, legion face-masked rescuers and soldiers, TV crews and composed aid workers, random young gawkers in their motorcycle helmets to shade the sun and victims' families huddled at the edge of what remains of the basketball court. This is what's happening now. The electricity is here. I plug in.

Only the broad tin roof, attached to steel girders, has retained its basic shape in the collapse and the following searches. Everything else is a concrete anthill. The excavator perches on top of the pile of rubble it's already pulled out and works down in the right hand corner of the ruins, where seven students are thought to have died descending stairs from the third floor listening laboratory. When the machine's diesel engine rumbles to a stop, and soldiers and orange-shirted search and rescue team members call for body bags, the younger watchers and cameramen surge to the top of the heap to have a look down into the hole. False alarm. This repeats several times. Cut engine. Surge. Nothing. Back to work. Through it, the families stick to a bench in a thin strip of shade at the back of the courtyard, and slurp noodles they've cooked over a portable burner in a breezeway along the alley out to the street. They're as far away as they can be and still be here.

A Western television reporter of no visible brand arrives to grill the college head, a squat, dowdy woman fidgeting in front of the camera and squeezing her fingers together so hard they look like they will pop. Why did classes resume here in 2007, even though the building was damaged in that earthquake? the reporter wants to know. The college head says she was told the building was safe. Then why did it fall down and others didn't? she's asked. It had something to do with how the earthquake arrived, she replies.

The questions sound shrill amongst the Indonesian copers and the watchers, neither group feeling particularly analytical or demanding of the college chief. She sits right among the families on the bench. Nobody wants to ask why the cracks in the building were just filled in after the two earthquakes in 2007, or why students were encouraged to come back despite their misgivings about the structure. Nobody wants to think about how ironic it is that you send your child to get a future here, but the operators don't have the decency to make sure the building will survive the next year. No one wants to show that sort of caustic emotion because you don't do that in Indonesia. Right now, it's either you died, or your kinsmen did, or you somehow escaped and you're looking in. You accept your lot.

A soldier descends from the pile carrying a black backpack gingerly in his rubber-gloved hands, and he takes it to a round mother sitting peacefully in the shade of a solitary tree at the edge of the basketball court. He unzips it to show her what is inside and the stench of decomposing flesh is soon so overpowering, 20 meters away, that I pull my T-shirt over my nose. The watchers go toward it, dozens of them clotting around her, holding their phones over the center of the circle and snapping pictures. A local Catholic priest, who knew some of the kids buried in the rubble, looks at the crowd and says, softly, "They like to see the victim. I don't think people should do it. But they like to watch a bad situation. Car accidents, too. But they'll brag to other people – 'I saw it'." It's true that the young people watching, digging, driving ambulances and mugging for cameras are as charged by this moment as I've ever seen them.

It is a seeming eternity — the excavator swaps out for one with a magnet shovel, a Jakarta TV station goes live with some students who ran out of the building — before scrap wood barriers go up to clear a path from the rubble to the alleyway. The gawkers are sent behind the line, and the families, led by stout Batak mothers from the neighboring province of Riau stand up to have a look. There's an expectant hush. Then some shouts from the knot of soldiers and rescue workers. And then the first black bag comes out, soldiers scrambling to get purchase on its hand loops and seams, as if it's bulkier and heavier than they expected. Six of them finally carry it down awkwardly, the victims' feet clearly pressing against one end of the bag and pointing skyward. People hoist cell phones and I raise my own pocket camcorder above the crowd, as the recovery group labors by and out to the street. Another body follows quickly. As the third body bag goes out to a waiting ambulance, a Riau family nearby learns from one of the bearers that it is theirs and they follow silently, to travel with it to the hospital. After the fourth, a soldier brings a tan and black fake leather purse into the crowded breezeway to the father of another student from Riau. She was Nova Situmorang. Nova, as in, *starts with N*. As in *not Nafitri*, my translator. Nova's dad confirms that's her purse, and the confirmation half paralyzes him. He has tears in his eyes but they're frozen. Only with help does he shuffle 10 meters through the milling crowd, his facemask drooping pathetically around his chin, to plop down on his family mat.

When he catches his breath, he and the family rouse and wade through to a waiting ambulance. Just as he's climbing in, there's some commotion among the rescue workers in the sea of watchers. Nova's dad is pulled back from the ambulance and told to wait. She's not been recovered yet.

At that moment he stops, closes his eyes and lets out a long, deep bellow from somewhere down in his gut. It's unmistakable anger and frustration, built during this long, two-day vigil, and it hangs a moment over all of us. A cry for earthquakes and buildings that collapse in them. For cowardly leaders. Basketball courts turned into waiting lounges. Stale noodles and prying onlookers.

For purses that reek of death. Most of all, for the capricious way that his daughter could be at school, or not at school. In this ambulance or still in the rubble. On that measly, broken piece of dry erase board. Or not on it.

Among a nation of champion copers, of people resigned to deal with whatever comes their way, he's not coping right now. The question is, will this anger be infectious and draw in others in Padang? Will they finally tire of feeling like their lives are hanging at the end of a very thin thread? As a journalist in Padang says, before this earthquake nobody knew they had a right to be safe. But there are glimmers of change.

***

It's an Irishman who nudges people along.

In mid-January of 2010, after the final death toll has reached 1,100 and people all over the city and countryside huddle out the rainy season in the cobbled remains of their homes, geologist John McCloskey and colleagues publish a short letter in a British science journal that essentially says the city hasn't seen the worst. Nothing has changed for the better on the megathrust fault under the Mentawai Islands, and their measurement of stress in the region shows that the earthquake in September may have even cranked up levels of stress under the island of Siberut. "The threat of a great, [magnitude] 8.5, tsunamigenic earthquake on the Mentawai patch is unabated," they write. An article about McCloskey's findings published by the French newswire *Agence France Presse* reminds readers that in March 2005, he and colleagues also showed how the Aceh-Andaman quake had increased stress to the south under Nias and Southern Simeulue. Just weeks later, the heavy earthquake struck there. By the time the news story here in 2010 is translated and gets into Indonesian newspapers and websites, McCloskey's warning that nothing on the fault has changed has morphed into a 'prediction'. The scientist's apparent clairvoyance in 2005 is offered up again and again. In the January 18 edition of the *Padang Ekspres*, under the two-column headline that translates to 'PADANG NOT SAFE YET', his admission that the timing of the future quake was still uncertain and that it could take decades to hit has been edited out. But the fact that he and his team were able to 'predict' the 2005 earthquake and now are 'predicting' one again is deemed 'strange'.

In Padang, people are still moderately freaked out two weeks later, when I pay a visit, not least because a crackpot website called nextearthquake.com has also predicted big earthquakes in late January and February. Arya, the professional who's been itching to get out of Padang, has spent the last two weeks securing a transfer to a new job in Jakarta. A banker who's taken a job high in Bukittinggi and kept his family in neighboring Riau province asks by text, "Do you think Padang is safe yet?" Many people in Padang nervously ask that same question over and over, invoking McCloskey, who's now a household name. Others who are well aware of the continuing threat wish that McCloskey and the scientists would hush up. "He doesn't know how it feels to be in an area after a quake with a woman and two kids and recover psychologically and rebuild your house. He's creating stress," says Aim Zein, the radio station owner who's been rebuilding his collapsed carport and the toppled brick wall around his property.

Blood pressure is rising across town. While some banks and shop owners have plunged headlong into demolition, the reconstruction effort looks hopelessly slow to families and government workers. Schools are carrying on in tents. Many neighborhoods, like Aim Zein's, still don't have water service. More than 180,000 houses in the city and the surrounding province need help rebuilding and the government has so far aided 7,000. Pariaman, the city of 50,000 closest to the epicenter, is still in the worst shape. Every second house looks a total loss. Mostly built from unreinforced brick walls and glazed by a thin coat of cement, they buckled in the quake, shearing off huge sections or toppling over in a heap.

Homeowners waiting for their assistance grow increasingly angsty over a plan to pay out the money to neighborhood groups of a dozen to two dozen stricken families. People's tendency to debate everything — in the Minang style — dims that plans' prospects. And it's worsened by the fact that people seem to have become even more selfish and edgy around town since the earthquake, says one mother I visit. At her ramshackle rented shack 20 meters from the family's old battered house and rotting along the floor boards, she lapses into a curse-laden rant about her son's plan to buy a new computer for university, "at a time like this!"

"Don't look any farther than me," she says, pulling out an unfiltered cigarette, unabashed about taboos on women smoking. "I'm much more sensitive and irritable now than I ever was." But to realize any hope of putting the old house back together, she'll have to swallow hard and join a group of her neighbors — "a bunch of smart alecs".

Some of the most serious soul searching about the future is in Pondok, where Chinese shop owners are prolonging rebuilding in light of the earthquake 'prediction'. Their older shophouses were heavily damaged, and many owners have the money and connections to cut loose of Padang and go elsewhere. The savvier bunch among 20,000 or so Chinese in Padang, these entrepreneurs are also the lifeblood of the wider city, running everything from small grocery stores right up to the big cinnamon and palm oil conglomerates. Padang's Chinese generally avoided the overt violence of those in other cities during riots that precipitated the fall of strongman Suharto in 1998 — which began in Jakarta and then spread to other cities and forced Chinese shopowners all over Indonesia into hiding. But they cite other slights: not being able to get space in the newer malls is one. And the earthquake is reinforcing their sense of isolation; many families say they were left out of city aid distributions of noodles and water. (In reality, a lot of neighborhoods aren't getting any aid, not just Pondok. A handful of Chinese community organizations, supported by wealthy donors in Jakarta, Hong Kong and Malaysia, are stepping in decisively by offering food and water and substantial donations to help members rebuild their homes and shops.)

An Amway home products distributor, whom I'd met over at Hotel Padang just after the quake, says that with so many of her friends staying in Jakarta and Pekanbaru in Riau, and with McCloskey's news, she's wary of investing more of their own money — not money paid by insurance, which they didn't have — in a new shophouse that might be wrecked by an imminent earthquake. Her husband is even mulling a rumor that Sumatra will split in two and one side will sink into the ocean. Johnson Chandra and his father have found a new spot to operate their pharmacy, and they're still keen to rebuild a stronger shophouse on the old site, with closely monitored construction. But their neighbor, whom they need to join the reconstruction, is waffling. And Johnson says he even noticed a drop in activity downtown after the news about future earthquakes arose.

Young people complain that with the three major malls closed for damage, Padang is a 'Dead City'. All the dark hulking abandoned structures in town make the place seem even more listless than usual after dark, even creepy. Even the foreign surfers are suffering: Christina Fowler and Chris Scurrah split up after the earthquake, leaving the Batang Arau café unresurrected. The whole place isn't good for another four or five years, says Arya, the professional heading off for Jakarta. What if the Dead City becomes a long-term reality?

Things seem to boil over in two days of lively demonstrations outside Mayor Fauzi Bahar's house, led by produce sellers from the destroyed downtown market who've been moved into temporary tent stalls in a nearby street. Fauzi's now running for governor of West Sumatra, and his potential opponents have no doubt paid some of the protesters. But they're joined by some earthquake victims still waiting for their housing reconstruction money, and the anger looks unmistakably genuine on the nightly TV reruns: people throw Molotov cocktails and rocks at police, and run onto Fauzi's front lawn (he's in Jakarta at the time), before police turn the water cannons on the crowd. Seven demonstrators and police end up in the hospital.

"Somebody needs to calm us down," says one Minang mother.

But that's looking increasingly difficult and beyond the scope of even the smoothest of orators, because nothing anyone can say right now would do the trick. Despite the hype and skewing of McCloskey's warnings, there is truth at the core of them, and people know it. "I can see where he's coming from," Aim Zein allows. A Chinese businessman in Pondok says "Everybody's been watching the scientists on TV for years now and they know exactly what they're saying." The issue is that Padang knows too much and it's experienced too much to slip back into the same fatalist groove. That's an awful, sinking feeling, that makes talking to people downright depressing at times. What they need right now is something transformative.

***

Through the thick emotional haze settling in over Padang, Helmi, a professor of agriculture at Andalas University, finds me. He is small, with a shock of white hair and a white mustache that curls down at the corners, and he's been given an impossible job. Just after the earthquake, the city asked him to head a council of local academics charged with injecting life back into the city. They responded with a plan for reorienting the city away from the water by developing new areas and rebuilding city office buildings out near the eastern ring road, known as the Bypass Road. The initiative promised to revive open-air markets outside of the center, and looked to move bus lines inland from coastal arteries as well. It would also place tsunami escape towers on some of the new buildings that have to be reconstructed closer to the water, and widen key avenues heading away from the water. When I first heard about these ideas a few months back, I was skeptical, along with many longtime observers of Padang. But Helmi insists the plan is not simply hot air, of the variety Mayor Fauzi has been known to blow.

Helmi and the team of experts spoke to the entire city council on four different occasions. "We told them that if they didn't adopt something like this, they would lose the trust of the voters," he says. The council extended its budgeting three weeks past the normal end-of-the-year deadline and earmarked $6 million for new projects, the first being a seismically-safe central market with an evacuation platform on top. Helmi also joined the head of the council and Mayor Fauzi in a special trip to Jakarta to ask for the national legislature to fund their new city plan. The process for realizing the vision — altering city spatial and development plans and winning support from a demoralized public — looks hairy. "It's going to be tougher than getting the money," say Helmi. "Look at the demos outside Fauzi's house!" he says, breaking into gentle cackles. But the city can't simply be patched together. In recent days, the makeshift markets have been knee-deep in floodwater from drains in ill repair. "The leadership style of Fauzi and the unresponsiveness of government is mixing with the hardships poor people are facing," he says, soberly.

Helmi insists things are moving. The new central market building looks possible by the end of the year. As if on cue, a pair of Helmi's young helpers arrive at the restaurant where we're having dinner and hand him two documents to sign: the plans for the relocation of government that are headed off to Jakarta, and a request for engineering design bids for the new central market.

Afterwards, I ask to see his two-story house, which he built to withstand earthquakes in 1997, using little more than intuition. He asked the contractor to put in extra rebar and tied the walls to the main roof timbers to create a sturdy box of a frame. He mixed large gravel into the concrete for better strength, and wherever there was a long wall or big open ceiling he added an extra column or a bracing structure — a toilet, in one case. "I had no engineering background," says Helmi, who earned his PhD in agricultural policy in England. "But I knew about the big earthquakes in Padang Panjang in 1926 [along the landward Sumatran fault]. And I just thought 'What if?'"

In the September quake, most of the soaring, neoclassical houses around his wealthy neighborhood, with gaudy columns and two-story windows, sloughed off huge chunks of masonry and collapsed their roofs — his next-door neighbor rained a piece of his outer wall into Helmi's yard. Many neighbors have deserted for Jakarta, leaving their broken houses dark. Walking under his own low roofline and into his square family room that rises to two stories, Helmi victoriously shows off his limited toll: hairline cracks in his wall paint and the busted computer hard drive that shimmied off his desk in the living room and which he duct-taped back together. "It still works!" he cries delightfully.

After the quake, he and his wife Rini, a food technology professor at Andalas, started an emergency kitchen over on the main thoroughfare of Agus Salim, in Rini's family shophouse (a 1960s building that also survived fine). They made 500 rice and curry bundles the first day, with some relatives' help. Then, they convinced a local radio station to solicit contributions and tell the needy where to go for food, and the trade soared. "We made 4,000 *bunkus* in one day," Helmi cackled. "No, 3,800," says Rini, firmly. She's joined us from a back room, covered with a simple headscarf.

After a week of making meals, the couple switched to building temporary shelters around Pariaman, the town closest to the epicenter. They concentrated on families that were elderly or had young children, and asked the families and relatives to build a simple frame out of what wood they could find. When it was finished, Rini and Helmi delivered cement for a foundation, plywood for the walls and the makings of a tin roof. The community put the pieces together. "We thought maybe 10 or 20 houses was all, but when I saw them going up I thought more, more!" Rini exclaims. Now they're at over 100 houses. "I like this job and I'm happy to do it. I'm happier sometimes than the people receiving houses." They've now hired a man in Pariaman to construct the temporary homes, giving him tools and paying him $75 a house. He and his crew are being hired out by other groups to do building work. "It's opening up opportunities for them!" Helmi says, laughing heartily again.

I get the sense, between Helmi and Rini's jovial plunge into the overwhelming rebuilding effort and his straitlaced assessment of the work the city is digging into, that the grassroots work that began with people like Patra and Febrin after Aceh is spreading, and it's also beginning to link up with more sophisticated city-wide planning. Amidst the widespread destruction and the morale laid low, Helmi and his colleagues are seeing issues holistically, as interconnected things that need to be solved together, not bandaged over. The chronic issues of congestion around the downtown market are also exacerbating the tsunami threat, less than a kilometer from the water. Solve one and you alleviate the other. Build multi-story market buildings and schools and hospitals that will withstand a heavy earthquake and you protect some of your crucial community centers and provide a way for people to climb away from tsunami waves.

***

As 2010 rolls forward, action from community groups and coalitions piles on. The Red Cross spreads out its disaster education to more communities, Kogami is expanding programs to get mosques to announce information after a tsunami on their ubiquitous, generator-powered loudspeakers and local journalists are starting new radio stations and newspapers dedicated to natural disasters. An American-led group gets funding from the reinsurance giant Swiss Re to build an artificial tsunami escape hill somewhere in town. Meanwhile, the German technical cooperation agency convinces the city to start communicating with people on emergency radio bands that will automatically come through to modified FM radios. And the city finally gets the map of the tsunami danger areas developed by consensus from scientists.

In what might be the most innovative venture, IDEP Foundation, a Bali-based environmental group that once created videos and materials used by Kogami and SurfAid, draws in a famous Minang star of Indonesian soaps (*sinetrons* in the local parlance) to spearhead a West Sumatran airwave onslaught aimed at convincing people and contractors to rebuild their homes stronger.

In one slick commercial, she traverses the province surveying the damage before wrapping up with a line that has become a mantra of other groups in quake-torn places across the world: "Earthquakes don't kill people, buildings do." *Sinetron* gives way to nuts and bolts: all the spots, talk shows and adverts point locals to new guide materials flooding the community, including a painstaking step-by-step video IDEP shot of builders tying off steel rebar, digging deep foundation trenches and the rest of the behind-the-scenes work needed for a quake-resistant house. But there is no doubt this effort is trying to strike deeper at the cultural level:

one staff member teams up with local artists and musicians around the province to write songs and paint murals and sift the message down into the Minang psyche.

Slowly, the efforts begin to pay dividends by the first anniversary of the quake. In one Padang neighborhood of 105 houses, nearly all of them badly damaged, home owners coughed up the extra $400 for quality materials and extra labor to build back 60 percent of their houses using new methods.

Other areas are still in transitional shelters. And among government buildings and schools, the money and approvals are spotty as well. About 400 of 1,000 destroyed schools in the province have risen back stronger, thanks to a large infusion of cash from domestic and foreign aid groups. The other half are soldiering on in tents or mosques.

While many government offices still sit in rubble or stacked like blocks, the main provincial office building begins rising on the anniversary with a blueprint to make it quake resistant and to provide a tsunami escape on its top floors for about 3,500 people.

Already, a quake resistant school built from scratch in Aim Zein's neighborhood has an escape platform on its roof.

Helmi and city officials acknowledge it will be years, maybe even a decade before the government buildings finish along the Bypass Road and the transport and commercial action shifts there and to other revitalized outlying centers.

Nobody in Padang has yet shown himself or herself to be the leader who can ensure that shift will happen. Nor is there someone creatively and comprehensively leading the charge on informing people and keeping them interested and updated on tsunamis over the next generation. So far the issues have proven too complex for one person, or one department, or one organization to lead it all imaginatively. What is rushing in to fill the vacuum is a patchwork of programs and structures and ideas.

Will all the efforts add up to a lasting, protective armor? A tsunami will tell.

Right now, with each incremental step like a sturdy escape platform, local leaders gesture to citizens that they're not just avoiding a repeat of the last disaster but also taking a long view toward the tsunami. The city is also cementing into place a reminder and a conversation starter. It's like an old piece of coral thrown into a rice paddy, or a safe house built high above a village, or a monument marking a tsunami's historical flood.

Perhaps 10 years from now, when a child passes that funny shaped school in Padang for the first time, she will wonder and ask about it. Any adult will, hopefully, be able to respond with a story. A long one, really. It starts with a single word from Japan, stretches across the length of Sumatra, arcs backward through the island's rich past, plumbs the depths of human nature, and just might, under the right conditions, leave the child in the right frame of mind. Alert to reality, not scared of it.

Afterword

Every time I return to Singapore from Padang, slip into a comfortable, air-conditioned taxi at sleek Changi Airport and slide up the smooth, wide expressway toward the city center, I exhale a sigh of relief. Singapore has its own challenges — "no romance", as one of my favorite university professors in Padang put it — but safety is not one of them, at least at first blush. The place is a relatively benign geologic landscape, with none of the earthquake faults and volcanoes that bedevil its big neighbor to the south. And it's also run by some of the most obsessive and well-trained planners on the earth. Not much has been left to chance. Rapid transit, a 21st century freeway system and more than 25,000 taxis float the city's densely packed 5.5 million people with little event each day. Savings accounts are mandated. Gamblers can be excluded from casinos by their families. New industry is constantly being attracted to keep employment full. And the homeless are whisked off to transitional shelters.

The same well-educated talent that has set up the system has also turned its attention outward to look at environmental threats to the cherished prosperity.* *Kiasu* — that fear of loss — never sleeps. The state's development of alternatives to sourcing water from regional rival Malaysia —from purifying run-off and sewer effluent to investing in desalinization and new freshwater reservoirs — tends to get the most attention.

But planners and scientists have also recently been studying the impacts of threats from potential tsunamis generated by the fault offshore of Sumatra, as it extends toward India in the Andaman Sea, and also the fault called the Manila Trench, west of the Philippines. The latest consensus is that the island of Singapore is sheltered too well to see much impact. Sumatra buffers it from most of the offshore fault there, and what little exposed, open water exists in the Malacca Strait is shallow, which would slow down and diminish any tsunami waves. On the eastern side, a tsunami from the Manila Trench would need ten hours to cross the South China Sea to Singapore, before it again would hit shallow waters. Some west facing beaches could see 0.7-meter waves from a magnitude 9 earthquake on the Manila Trench. The national environment agency has developed a plan to evacuate areas of the popular Sentosa Island tourist district and parks in the Jurong and West Coast areas. Given the small area to evacuate and the long lead-time to do it, this seems doable.

Global warming, however, lurks as a murkier threat. Singapore leaders have been closely monitoring projections for global sea level rise, which are of obvious concern on an island city-state where the parliament building and main financial district are at two and three meters above sea level, respectively. Unabated, the

---

* *Singapore's per capita GDP was $50,000 in 2009, higher than the United States and fourth in the world.*

sea level rise could put the lowest lying areas along the waterfront at risk under extreme high tide, like the freak four meter tide that inundated Changi airport in 1974. It would also make the city more difficult to drain after a large monsoon. Newer armaments and flood control gates are built to accommodate a half meter of sea level rise, which the United Nations' climate change panel suggested in 2007 would be the worst case scenario over the next 100 years. Developments on reclaimed land also must be built at 1.25 meters above mean high tide to brace for the increase. And the government has contracted with Dutch engineers to design new dykes and walls to keep out the sea, should some areas of the city become permanently below sea level, as in Amsterdam or the Italian city of Venice. Still, sea level rise this century is already accelerating faster than imagined even in 2007. Scientists have said that half a meter now looks certain by the end of the century, and that many areas will likely see one meter of rise by 2100.

If sea level rise is proving tough to pin down, then rainfall fluctuation under climate change is close to impossible to predict. Some projections have Singapore losing net rainfall, others have it increasing 15% by the end of the century. Meanwhile regional countries, which Singapore depends on for food, may be facing prolonged droughts in moodier climates. One Massachusetts Institute of Technology study last year had Thailand's rice yield dropping anywhere from 3% to 13% by the end of the century, depending on how much the Earth warms. It's counterintuitive to think of permanently drenched Southeast Asia facing prolonged drought, but some historians think a warming period and drought around 1200 helped bring down the kingdom of Angkor Wat, in today's Cambodia. And the Singapore government considers it a real threat. In early 2010, government staff held meetings behind closed doors with scientists to discuss how warming-induced drought would fuel food insecurity and general instability in the region.

On the wetter end of the spectrum, Singaporeans already had a preview of things to come in June and July 2010. In the usual dry season, the city was pummeled by unprecedented monsoons. In one two-hour period, Singapore recorded 100 millimeters of rain. Cars floated away on residential streets. Surprised shoppers on the famed Orchard Road — the same one where visitors from the wilds of Indonesia or the Philippines like to go for the creature comforts of window shopping and a movie — had to be rescued from the thigh-deep floods by civil defense force members. Even the country's highly respected founding father and die-hard government proponent, Lee Kuan Yew, had to admit (obliquely) that Singapore had failed to manage the situation properly. "How can you say that the response is sufficient?" he said. It was as close as he'd gotten to criticizing the government run by his son, Lee Hsien Loong, in years.

But that response and the images of people being rescued in suits and stylish skirts confirms how city residents are deeply insulated from the elements. Both sides — citizens and government officials — take for granted that the state will completely protect its people under any threat. An increasingly complex drainage network sweeps away water from a city that, as older residents can attest, used to flood regularly in the 1960s. As a result, few bother to think about floods outside government offices today.

That attitude may have to change, even in relatively safe places and even in Singapore. In more extreme climates, deluges

like those in 2010 will no longer be 50-year events, as Singapore's
environment minister called them. A more robust SMS warning
system in the city and added drains may help, but people might
also begin to take care of themselves. Residents along the upper
Singapore River have begun to expect flooding and learned to take
simple steps, like moving their cars off the street to elevated car
parks. A wider group of residents and business owners in the river
valley will need to develop these sorts of instincts about flooding
when those heavy, abnormal rains set in. There'll also be financial
incentives to living more attuned to flooding: insurers have
already said they will raise flood insurance rates in areas affected
by the 2010 storms. Previously, flood insurance came free or at a
nominal cost.

As Singapore and other modern, asphalt jungles reconnect with
instincts about natural hazards it will serve their citizens beyond
their borders, as well. There were 327 million foreign arrivals in the
Asia-Pacific region, during travel's last peak in 2007, and budget
airline competition promises more growth. So much of travel from
Asian cities to other countries takes people to simpler places, away
from the hustle and bustle, or for immersion into the crowded
shop streets of another culture. We're vigilant about some things
— pickpockets, moneychangers, steep prices. But how much do
we ever think about unseen natural hazards?

It's possible to think of a tourist trail that hop scotches across
Asia and is dotted by a different sort of 'hot spots' — getaways
that also have hazards lurking. It starts with the earthquake-prone
highlands of India's Ladakh and moves along the fault-ridden
Himalayan front into oft-visited Nepal and Bhutan, through the
temple-studded outskirts of Mandalay, atop a fault now quiet for

140 years, on to the up-and-coming trekking villages in Myanmar's Shan area, on into China's southeast, where the casino jungle of Macau may sit at high tsunami risk from earthquakes along the Manila Trench. Hong Kong's low-lying districts are susceptible to a substantial magnitude 6 quake like the two in nearby mainland China that shook it in the 1960s. Hopping over to Taiwan and its typhoon-drenched and alluring national parks, the trail moves down through the seismically-active, volcano- and typhoon- exposed north of the Philippines, including highly touted tourist zones like Misibis, and down into Indonesia through the earthquake-prone diving mecca of Manado, into Sumatra and Java and out to the South Pacific Islands, where earthquake and tsunami threats were realized in September 2009.

The Pacific Asia Tourism Association (PATA), the region's largest industry organization, had slated a tourism and development conference for Samoa in November 2009, until the late September tsunami, up to three-meters high, tore through resort-heavy Upolu, the capital island in the country. The organization quickly changed gears, establishing its first-ever disaster relief fund and scheduling an impromptu reconstruction seminar in Samoa. "We were looking at how to rebuild infrastructure instead," says Dale Lawrence, the communications director at PATA's Bangkok headquarters.

Tourism operators are just waking up to the idea that they need to act on that kind of long-term information in protecting their guests. "It's fair to say that certain destinations around the Asia-Pacific region don't take enough measures to prepare for this stuff," says Dale Lawrence with the tourism association. And it's fair to say tourists are just waking up, too.

A little knowledge goes a long way. In Thailand, during the

tsunami, it was some of the foreigners that did the saving. Surfers and boat captains headed for high ground, recognizing strange tide-like movements. And nearly everyone now knows the story of visiting 10-year-old English girl Tilly Smith, 10,000 kilometers from home, who'd learned about tsunamis in her geography class back home. After earthquakes, her teacher told her, a strange sea would indicate something wasn't right. On Phuket Island in Thailand, on Boxing Day, "I was on the beach and the water started to go funny. There were bubbles and the tide went out all of a sudden," Smith told a reporter. "I recognized what was happening and had a feeling there was going to be a tsunami."

Through her parents, she passed the information on to hotel authorities and they cleared the beach of more than 100 people. Nothing more than basic, schoolgirl knowledge and a sort of childish keenness for noticing odd things saved those people that day. We would do well to get that keenness back, in these urbanizing, warming, globe-trotting days.

Notes on Sources

Many sections of the book follow first hand reporting and interviews; for the remaining text, I've noted main sources for information.

1.

Kerry Sieh's account of the first of his trips through the Sumatran islands in January 2005 is at the Caltech Today website: www.today.caltech.edu/today/story-display?story_id=5903

A link to the 2005 video from the Acehnese photographer Hasyim is at www.usc.edu/dept/tsunamis/2005/tsunamis/041226_indianOcean/sumatra/tsunami_indo_web.mov.

Many websites advance all or part of the military conspiracy theories related to the tsunami. The story 'US Had Advance Warning of Tsunami: Canadian Professor', *The Daily Times*, January 3, 2005, raises most of the issues (www.dailytimes.com.pk/default.asp?page=story_3-1-2005_pg7_37). Unfortunately, it looks like collective negligence, not subterfuge, was the cause for no warning here. See short explanation in chapter 8.

The Thai scientist's warning is described in 'His Calls Ignored, Thai Meteorologist Now Plays Key Role' (*The Wall Street Journal Asia*, January 10, 2005 AI).

A transcript of Sieh's conversation from the February 13, 2005 episode of *60 Minutes Australia* is available at www.sixtyminutes.ninemsn.com.au/stories/richardcarleton/259246/the-next-wave.

2.

Columnist Thomas Friedman put it best three months after Katrina when he said: "If ours were a parliamentary system, Mr. Bush would have had to resign." See 'George Bush's Third Term', *New York Times*, November 23, 2005, www.select.nytimes.com/2005/11/23/opinion/23 friedman.html?ref=thomaslfriedman.

Various media were picking up the Sichuan story about angry parents, activists and 'tofu dregs' schools, including the *Chinese Digital Times* in 'China Detains Quake School Critic', June 18, 2008 (www. chinadigitaltimes.net/2008/06/china-detains-quake-school-critic/) and the *BBC* in 'China Reins in Quake School Fury', June 3, 2008 (http:// news.bbc.co.uk/2/hi/asia-pacific/7434054.stm).

The Premier's resignation was widely reported in Asia, including by the *New York Times*, 'Prime Minister of Taiwan Quits over Typhoon Response', September 7, 2009 (www.nytimes.com/200909/08/world/ asia/08taiwan.html?_r=2).

See this summation of the Nargis aid backup by Belanger, Judie et. al., 'Negotiating Humanitarian Access to Cyclone-Affected Areas in Myanmar', *Humanitarian Exchange Magazine*, Issue 41 (December 2008) (www.odihpn.org/report.asp?id=2964).

The Munich Re annual reports from 2005 and 2008 detail the industry's losses (www.munichre.com). The World Bank lists Israel's GDP in 2009 as just over $202 billion.

The United Nations International Strategy for Disaster Reduction Secretariat reported that 780,000 people were killed between 2000 to the end of 2009 in its newsbrief 'Earthquakes Caused the Deadliest Disasters in the Past Decade', January 28, 2010 (www.unisdr.org/ news/v.php?id=12470). The Haiti earthquake in early 2010 put the cumulative death toll at over 1 million.

James Jackson details cities building upon ruins in Iran in 'Fatal Attraction: Living with Earthquakes, the Growth of Villages into Megacities, and Earthquake Vulnerability in the Modern World', Philosophical Transactions of the Royal Society, Vol. 364 (2006), pp. 1911–1925). 'With Capital at High Risk of Quakes, Iran Weighs Moving It to a Safer Place' from the *New York Times* (January 6, 2004) notes adobe building practices in Iran.

Roger Bilham maps out urban risks globally in 'Seismic Future of Cities', *Bulletin of Earthquake Engineering*, Volume 7, No. 4 (September 2, 2009) pp. 839–887 (www.springerlink.com/content/m88166m8x217p0u3).

The United Nations' estimate of 200 million environmental migrants by 2050 is highlighted in the *Science Daily* article 'Environmental Migrants: UN Meeting Aims to Build Consensus on Definitions, Support, Protection', October 8, 2008 (www.sciencedaily.com/releases/2008/10/081008151106.htm).

Sound investments in prevention are described in the Red Cross/Red Crescent's *World Disaster Report 2009* (Geneva: International Federation of Red Cross/Red Crescent, 2009, p. 88).

An international team found Chile's building practices sound: 'Geo-Engineering Reconnaissance of the February 27, 2010 Maule, Chile Earthquake', *GEER Association Report* No. GEER-022 Version 1: April 15, 2010 (www.geerassociation.org).

Success in Bangladesh with cyclone warnings is detailed by the United Nations in 'Bangladesh: Megaphones Save Thousands', November 23, 2007 (www.irinnews.org/Report.aspx?ReportId=75470) and in an article 'Myanmar's deadly daffodil' in *Nature Geoscience* online, July 20, 2008 (www.nature.com/naturegeoscience)

Evacuation failures in New Orleans are documented in the congressional report 'Failure of Initiative: Final Report of the Select Bipartisan Committee to Investigate the Preparation For and Response to Hurricane Katrina' (Washington: US Government Printing Office, February 15, 2006, pp.111–117, www.gpoaccess.gov/katrinareport/mainreport.pdf). A report written by the Bangkok-based Asian Disaster Preparedness Center and Myanmese authorities suggests that Myanmar did get some warnings on the TV but people had no idea how big a storm surge to expect: 'Joint Rapid Situation Assessment Report: Status and Context of Four Coastal Townships in the Yangon and Ayeyarwady Divisions in Myanmar', May 2008, Bangkok, Thailand (www.adpc.net/v2007).

New York Times reporter Andy Revkin waded through the street-level issues in Istanbul in 'Disaster Awaits Cities in Earthquake

Zones', February 25, 2010 (www.nytimes.com/2010/02/25/science/earth/25quake.html?emc=eta1). Merapi's volcano communities were followed by *National Geographic* in 'Living with Volcanoes', January 2008 (www.ngm.nationalgeographic.com/2008/01/volcano-culture/andrew-marshall-text.html). John McPhee's book, *The Control of Nature* (New York: Farrar; Straus & Giroux, 1990) finds the Angelinos setting up house in front of future debris flows.

The debate after Aceh played out in a number of news stories. One good source was a *Der Spiegel* story, 'Would An Alert System Have Helped?', on January 11, 2005 (www.spiegel.de/international/0,1518,336307,00.html). Interviews with Kerry Sieh, Harald Spahn, Danny Natawidjaja, Brian Atwater helped flesh out the nature of the debate.

Fauzi, the early warning system director in Jakarta, detailed contributions to the warning system by other countries.

The "totally numb" comment comes from Aim Zein, the former consultant to the German warning system.

Matt Kaplan's story in *New Scientist*, 'When Animals Predict Earthquakes', Vol. 293, February 17, 2007 captures a lot of the sensory perception discussion around earthquakes and tsunamis (www.newscientist.com/article/mg19325911.800-when-animals-predict-earthquakes.html). *TIME* wrote about the phenomenon at Helice in 'Can Toads Predict Earthquakes?' (April 1, 2010, www.time.com/time/health/article/0,8599,1977090,00.html).

A story from *The Telegraph*, 'Did They Sense the Tsunami?', January 8, 2005 (www.telegraph.co.uk/technology/3337851/Did-they-sense-the-tsunami.html) picked up on the theory of Joseph Kirschvink about a tsunami escape response, based on his earlier paper, 'Earthquake Prediction by Animals: Evolution and Sensory Perception', *Bulletin of the Seismological Society of America*, Vol. 90, No. 2 (April 2000) pp. 312–323. On page 313, Kirschvink explains how bees' waggle language evolved from experimental behavior.

Examples of recent human evolution are touched on in the *New York Times* story, 'Adventures in Recent Human Evolution', July 20, 2010 (www.nytimes.com/2010/07/20/science/20adapt.html?pagewanted=2&emc=eta1).

Krakatau's tsunami heights and arrival times are here: Choi, B. H. et. al. 'Simulation of the trans-oceanic tsunami propagation due to the 1883 Krakatau volcanic eruption', *Natural Hazards and Earth System Sciences* (2003) Vol. 3: pp321–332.

The rate of tsunamis across the Asia-Pacific region is covered in Sidle, et. al. 'Interactions of Natural Hazards and Society in Austral-Asia: Evidence in Past and Recent Records', *Quaternary International*, (2004) pp. 118–119. Much of the historical accounts of the Japanese tsunamis, and the real and imagined portions of 'The Living God' comes from the fact-packed book, *The Orphan Tsunami of 1700 — Japanese Clues to a Parent Earthquake in North America* by Brian Atwater, Satoko Musimi-Rokkaku, Kenji Satake, Yoshinobu Tsuji, Kazue Ueda and David K. Yamaguchi (Seattle: UW Press, 2005). Julyan Cartwright and Hisam Nakamura also provided background and details on the earliest tsunamis and more about Lafcadio Hearn in 'A History of the Term and of Scientific Understanding in Japanese and Western Culture', *Notes & Records of the Royal Society* Vol. 62 (2008) pp. 151–166. For details about the Sanriku coast of northeast Honshu, I also drew on 'Public Education of Tsunami Disaster Mitigation and Rehabilitation Performed in Japanese Primary Schools' by Hideki Ohta, et. al. (*International Conference on Geotechnical Engineer for Disaster Mitigation and Rehabilitation*, J. Chu, Phoon and Young eds. Singapore: World Scientific, 2005). The Japanese tsunami and earthquake expert Fumihiko Imamura filled in some of the details of Sanriku culture.

Differentiated risks are explained in the opening section of Wisner, et. al. *At Risk: Natural Hazards, Peoples Vulnerability and Disasters* (London; New York: Routledge, 2004 pp. 9–26).

For a recent analysis of modern responses to tsunamis in Japan, I drew on a series of articles by American reporter Winston Ross following the 2004 tsunami, archived at the Oregon Department of Geology and Mineral Industries site (www.oregongeology.com/sub/earthquakes/oraltraditions.htm). Ross' articles explained how the Japanese were overwhelmed by war and economic issues after the 1896 tsunami. On engineering defenses see Wiegel, R. 'Tsunami Information Sources' *Science of Tsunami Hazards*, Vol. 25, No. 2 (2006).

Hamzah Latief articulated the blindness to tsunamis after independence. His 'Tsunami Catalogue and Zones in Indonesia', *Journal of Natural Disaster Science*, Vol. 22, No. 1 (2000) pp. 25–43, lists tsunamis in West Sumatra in 1904 and 1909 and a deadly tsunami off Aceh in 1964. Jean-Christophe Gaillard et. al. explore the Aceh conflict's impact on preparedness in 'Ethnic Groups' Response to the 26 December 2004 Earthquake and Tsunami in Aceh, Indonesia', *Natural Hazards* Vol. 47 (2008) pp. 17–38.

Most of the background on *smong* comes from the extensive study by Herry Yogaswara and Eko Yulianto's unpublished report for the Indonesian Institute of Sciences, 'Local Knowledge of Tsunami among the Simeulue Community, NAD'. It's available at the Jakarta Tsunami Information Center (www.jtic.org). Kerita, Tetsushi et. al. 'Regional Characteristics of Tsunami Risk Perception among the Tsunami Affected Countries in the Indian Ocean' (*Journal of Natural Disaster Science*, Volume 29, Number 1, 2007, pp. 29–38) documented the penetration of the *smong* story.

3.

The journey to Simeulue aboard the surf charters is partially documented on Patra Dewi's blog (www.patrarinadewi.multiply.com/tag/sro).

The *National Geographic* story, 'Tsunamis — Where Next?' appeared in the front Geographica section of the magazine's April 2005 edition.

Jeffrey Hadler describes the legend of the victorious buffalo in the second chapter of *Muslims and Matriarchs: Cultural Resilience in Indonesia Through Jihad and Colonialism* (Ithaca: Cornell University Press, 2008). Peggy Reeves Sanday interprets it as a victory for soft power in *Women at the Center: Life in a Modern Matriarchy* (Ithaca: Cornell University Press, 2002).

Anthony Reid's analysis of population shifts in Sumatra is in the third chapter of *Indonesian Frontier: Acehnese and Other Histories of Sumatra* (Singapore: Singapore University Press, 2005). He's lately begun to think of settlement more in terms of earthquakes and tsunamis. See his paper 'Seismology and Human Settlement: Global

Contexts for Local (Sumatra) Patterns', presented to the conference, Changing Nature of 'Nature': New Perspectives from Trandisciplinary Field Science, as part of the Global COE project of Kyoto University, Japan on December 16, 2009. Freek Colombijn follows the growth of Padang as a government center and education magnet in *Patches of Padang: A History of an Indonesian Town in the Twentieth Century and its Use of Urban Space* (Leiden: CNWS Publications, 1994).

Interviews with Patra Dewi, Febrin Ismail and David Lupo tracked the early work of tsunami volunteers. News reports documented tourism's decline after Aceh, including the story 'Earthquake, Tsunami Ruin W. Sumatra's Tourist Industry' by Syofiardi Bachyul Jb, *The Jakarta Post*, April 28, 2005. Tony Litwak's video 'Finding Higher Ground' caught some of the group's early work on tape (www.tonylitwak. com/48227.html).

4.

Kerry Sieh's early work in California is published in 'Pre-Historic Large Earthquakes Produced by Slip on the San Andreas Fault at Pallett Creek, California', which appeared in the *Journal of Geophysical Research*, Vol. 83, No. B8 (August 10, 1978) pp. 3907–3939. Frederick Taylor and colleagues' write-up their Vanuatu work here: 'Seismic Recurrence Intervals and Timing of Aseismic Subduction Inferred From Emerged Corals and Reefs of the Central Vanuatu (New Hebrides) Frontal Arc' in the *Journal of Geophysical Research*, Vol. 95, No. B1 (January 10, 1990) pp. 393–408.

The extensive survey of historical earthquakes in Sumatra and the surrounding region, 'Seismic History and Seismotectonics of the Sunda Arc', is by K. R. Newcomb and W. R. McCann in the *Journal of Geophysical Research*, Vol. 92, No. B1 (January 10, 1987) pp. 421–439.

Microatolls are summed up by T. P. Scoffin and D. R. Stoddart in 'The Nature and Significance of Microatolls', *Philosophical Transaction of the Royal Society of London Series B, Biological Sciences*, Vol. 284, No. 999, The Northern Great Barrier Reef (Nov. 14, 1978). Judy Zachariasen, et. al. also explains their growth behaviors in 'Submergence and Uplift Associated with the Giant 1833 Sumatran Subduction Earthquake:

Evidence from Coral Microatolls' in *Journal of Geological Research*, Vol. 104, No. B1 (Jan, 1999).

Anthony Reid outlines the reasons trade could move around, including due to natural disasters, in his introductory chapter in *Veranda on Violence: Background to the Aceh Problem* (Singapore: Singapore University Press, 2006).

For the historical accounts used here, I'm indebted, in addition to Danny Natawidjaja and Kerry Sieh, to a collection of historical and anthropological researchers who helped find, translate and interpret them as part of Natawidjaja et. al. 'Source Parameters of the Great Sumatran Megathrust Earthquakes of 1797 and 1833 Inferred from Coral Microatolls', *Journal of Geophysical Research*, Vol. 111 (2006) B06403. Juniator Tulis found many of the Dutch accounts and Maarten Schmidt translated them to English. Jenny Briggs translated German accounts, and Jeffrey Hadler gave historical interpretation.

The credible details of the 1797 tsunami come from the excerpts of du Puy, J. (1845) 'Een Aantekeningen Omtrent Vuurbergen en Aardbevingen op Sumatra', *Tijdsch. Neerland's Indie, 7*, and du Puy, J. (1847), 'Een Paar Aantekeningen Omtrent Vuurbergen en Aardbevingen op Sumatra', *Tijdsch. Neerland's Indie, 9.*

Christine Dobbin's detailed history of West Sumatra, *Islamic Revival in a Changing Peasant Economy* (London and Malmo: Curzon Press, 1983) encompasses the two earthquakes and gives just a few tantalizing details of their effects on life (there's no mention of tsunamis). See page 85 for a quick mention of building damage and page 98 for a discussion of swamps.

For the 1833 tsunami, it's du Puy, J. (1847) again, and also several aftermath accounts of volcanoes and rebellions from more sources translated in Natawidjaja: Boelhouwer, J. C., 'Herinneringen van Mijn Verblijf op Sumatra's Westkust Gedurende de Jaren, 1831–1834' (Gravenhage: Doorman, The Hague: 1841, pp. 175–176) and S. Miller en L. Horner. 'Fragmenten van de Reizen en Onderzoekingen in Sumatra' (Bijdr. t. de T. L. en Vk. (1) 3. 1855, pp. 25–27).

Freek Colombijn picked up the construction of new roads and neighborhoods in the 1840s in his book *Patches of Padang*, on page 59.

Anthony Reid, drawing on Dutch sources, called attention to the first two earthquakes in 1691 and 1697 in his paper 'Seismology and Human Settlement: Global Contexts for Local (Sumatra) Patterns'. Newcomb and McCann mention the other earthquakes and the few details in 'Seismic History'.

Underwater tableaus and other evidence of sinking are in Natawidjaja, Danny Hilman et. al. 'Interseismic deformation above the Sunda Megathrust recorded in coral microatolls of the Mentawai islands, West Sumatra', *Journal of Geophysical Research* Vol. 112 (2007) B02404.

The poster that Sieh's team handed out in the islands in 2004 is, as of this writing, available at the Sumatran Plate Boundary Project website (www.tectonics.caltech.edu/sumatra/public.html).

5.

Interviews with Patra Dewi, Febrin Ismail, Kerry Sieh and David Lupo are the primary source on Kogami's work.

The German agency for technical cooperation (GTZ) study of the evacuation in Padang is called 'Early Warning Experiences in Padang After the First Bengkulu Earthquake on 12 September 2007', and is available at www.gitews.org. Details of the 2007 quakes come from the paper by Konca, et. al. 'Partial Rupture of a Locked Patch of the Sumatra Megathrust During the 2007 Earthquake Sequence', *Nature* Vol. 456 (December 4, 2008). The tsunami height came from Borrero, Jose. C., et. al. 'The tsunami of 2007 September 12, Bengkulu province, Sumatra, Indonesia: post-tsunami field survey and numerical modeling', *Geophysical Journal International* (2009) volume 178, pp. 180-194.

Discussion about what's next in Sumatra is in Richard Kerr's 'Continuing Indonesian Quakes Put Seismologists on Edge', *Science*, Vol. 317 (September 21, 2007) pp. 1660–61. The nature of similar big faults comes from Brian Atwater and Kenji Satake's 'Long-Term Perspectives on Giant Earthquakes and Tsunamis at Subduction Zones', *Annual Review of Earth and Planetary Sciences* Vol. 35 (2007) pp. 349–374.

6.

Cecep Surbarya, et. al. 'Plate Boundary Deformation Associated with the Great Sumatra-Andaman Earthquake' *Nature*, Vol. 440 (March 2, 2006) pp. 46–51, shows how the seafloor was warped by the December 26, 2004 earthquake.

Franck Lavigne led the French and Indonesian crew that painstakingly recreated the Aceh tsunami, published in Lavigne et. al. 'Reconstruction of Tsunami Inland Propagation on December 26, 2004 in Banda Aceh, Indonesia, through Field Investigations', *Pure and Applied Geophysics*, Volume 166, Numbers 1–2 (February 2009) pp. 259–281. Lavigne and Co. are also behind a terrific documentary, *Tsunarisque*, that puts the study into vivid terms (see www.tsunarisque.cnrs.fr/en_index.htm).

Doak Cox explains Hokusai's wave in 'The Inappropriate Tsunami Wave Icon', *Science of Tsunami Hazards: The International Journal of the Tsunami Society*, Vol. 19, No. 2 (2001), pp. 87–91. Julyan Cartwright and Hisam Nakamura give more background on the history of tsunamis and the physics of the wave in 'Tsunami: A History of the Term and of Scientific Understanding of the Phenomenon in Japanese and Western Culture', *Notes and Records of The Royal Society*, Vol. 62, No. 2 (June 20, 2008), pp. 151–166.

David Lines' experience during the tsunami was documented by *CNN* (see www.edition.cnn.com/TRANSCRIPTS/0501/02/se.01. html) and by Cindy Wockner's article 'Swept Away' in *The Daily Telegraph* in Sydney, January, 1, 2005. He said in a brief conversation in 2010 that the experience had been exciting.

Jose Borrero's models in 'Tsunami Inundation Modeling for Western Sumatra', (*Proceedings of the National Academy of Sciences*, Vol. 103 No. 52 December 26, 2006 pp. 19673–19677) give a rough idea of what tsunamis would do in the Mentawai Islands. Information about the 1998 tsunami wave height came from the National Oceanic and Atmospheric Administration's event page (www.nctr.pmel.noaa. gov/PNG). A paper by Synolakis, et. al. 'The Slump Origin of the 1998 Papua New Guinea Tsunami', *Proceedings of the Royal Society of London*, Series A (2001) Volume 457, pp. 1–27, laid out the landslide explanation.

Surfer operator background and lore came from talks with Chris
Scurrah, Matt George, Tom Plummer, Amen Day, Mark Loughran,
Christina Fowler, Christie Carter, Alice Trend and numerous other
characters in Padang and the Mentawais.

See Lavigne et. al. for performance of berms in Banda Aceh in
2004.

7.

Kogami provided an update on projects in the city. The 2008 update on
the waterfront project, known sometimes as 'Padang Bay City', comes
from the Indonesian government's new service Antara, among others,
on August 4, 2008, 'Netherlands to Build Tunnel Maintaining Local
Tradition'. Minang population statistics from *Encyclopedia of Southeast
Asian Ethnography* (Delhi: Global Vision Publishing House, 2004) p. 446.

Fauzi Bahar's record with social law is outlined in 'Padang Mayor
Defends Sharia as Good for Development' by Syofiardi Bachyul Jb
in *The Jakarta Post*, February 9, 2006). Election details came from
interviews with Padang journalists.

Taufik Abdullah lays out the basis for conflict in Minangkabau
culture in his paper 'Adat and Islam: An Examination of Conflict
in Minangkabau', *Indonesia*, Vol. 2 (October 1966) pp. 1–24.
He addresses how Islamic law appears in the Tambo in 'Tambo,
Kaba, and History: Tradition and the Historical Consciousness of
the Minangkabau' in Walk in *Splendor: Ceremonial Dress and the
Minangkabau* (Anne and John Summerfield, eds., Los Angeles: UCLA
Fowler Museum of Cultural History, 1999: pp. 334–39). Hadler's
take on Imam Bondjol's change of heart is in *Muslims and Matriarchs*,
pages 20-28. The whole book, really, is about the influx of new ideas
and their accommodation in West Sumatra, with some highlights on
page 139. Abdullah also takes this up in 'Tambo'. Christine Dobbin
suggests Islamists' reform helped grow advantageous coffee trade in
Islamic Revival in a Changing Peasant Economy (London and Malmo:
Curzon Press, 1983).

Sanday's *Women at the Center* explains division of property on page
19 and the proverb about nature on page 23.

What did the Lisbon earthquake and tsunami mean in the West? A whole library's worth has been written on this subject. Both Susan Hough and Roger Bilham's *After the Earth Quakes: Elastic Rebound on an Urban Planet* (New York: Oxford University Press, 2006) and J. Z. de Boer and Donald Sanders' *Earthquakes in Human History: The Far Reaching Effects of Seismic Disruptions* (Princeton: Princeton University Press, 2005) provided background on the events and the thoughts unleashed. William F. Fleming's reprint and analysis of Voltaire's poem in 'The Lisbon Earthquake', *New England Review* Vol. 26, No. 3 (2005) pp. 183–193, framed the big thinker's thinking.

Edgar Brightman's 'The Lisbon Earthquake: A Study in Religious Valuation', *American Journal of Theology*, Vol. 23, No. 4 (Oct. 1919) pp. 500–518 neatly summarizes the bigger thought picture from all points of view, including the English priesthood. The original piece from John Michell 'Conjectures Concerning the Cause, and Observations upon the Phaenomena of Earthquakes; Particularly of That Great Earthquake of the First of November, 1755, Which Proved So Fatal to the City of Lisbon, and Whose Effects Were Felt As Far As Africa, and More or Less throughout Almost All Europe', *Philosophical Transactions of the Royal Society* (1683–1775), Vol. 51 (1759–1760), pp. 566–634, is a classic of an early scientist grappling with phenomena.

Michael Dove suggests how we got here from 1755 in 'Perception of volcanic eruption as agent of change on Merapi volcano, Central Java' (*Journal of Volcanology and Geothermal Research* Vol. 172 (2008) pp. 329–337).

David Chester has been arguing for a more robust engagement of theology during and after disasters, by noting things like popular church masses around Italy's Mt. Etna in 'Theology and Disaster Studies: The Need for Dialogue', *Journal of Volcanology and Geothermal Research*, Vol. 146 (2005) pp. 319– 328. U. of Washington's Clark Lombardi helped with *hadith* interpretation.

Colleague Nafitri Darmali tracked the mayor's debate and sent me a brief write up by email.

The Jakarta Post reported the election returns in October 2008 (www.thejakartapost.com/news/2008/10/27/pan-candidates-win-regional-elections.html).

8.

Information on Mentawai movers comes from SurfAid's Ray Mathias, Kirk Willcox and the local NGO Citra Mandiri.

The coral uplifts for the island near Silabu come from initial work of Sieh's doctoral student Judy Zachariasen published in 'Submergence and Uplift Associated with the Giant 1833 Sumatran Subduction Earthquake'.

August Lett's tale has been told many times, including by Australian historian Glenn Reeves in 'History and Prehistory of the Mentawai Islands' at www.mentawai.org/histbackgr.htm.

The background about forest issues is outlined in Gerard Persoon's article 'Conflict over Trees and Waves' in *Geografiska Annaler. Series B, Human Geography*, Vol. 85, No. 4, Special Issue: Nature-Society Interactions on Islands (2003), pp. 253–264. The conversion of people in the Mentawais and elsewhere is discussed by Gavin Jones, 'Religion and Education in Indonesia', *Indonesia*, Vol. 22 (October 1976), pp. 19–56. Statistics of conversion in the islands is on page 28.

The story of the young *kerei* comes from Reimar Schefolds' essay on pp. 105–06 in *Mentawai Shaman: Keeper of the Rainforest* by photographer Charles Lindsay (New York: Aperture, 1983).

Schefold personally passed on the first version of the watercourse spirit legend told here, while the second version, focused more on an 'earthquake' spirit, can be found in Koen Meyers and Puteri Watson's paper 'Legend, Ritual and Architecture', in *Indigenous Knowledge for Disaster Risk Reduction: Good Practices and Lessons Learned from Experiences in the Asia-Pacific Region*, International Strategy for Disaster Reduction (2008) pp. 17–22 (www.unisdr.org).

The description of settlement came through in interviews with villagers, as well as Koen Meyers, and SurfAid's Ray Mathias. Tom Plummer provided information about electricity in the islands and transitions at Berkat/Berimanua.

9.

Pranata and other Jakarta warning center officials gave the details on the December 26, 2004 interpretation during interviews.

The interview of Masni Fanshuri's English students on the Padang warning system came in May 2009.

The Pacific Tsunami Warning Center website gives a basic background on the center. The Orphan Tsunami and Atwater, Brian et. al. 'Surviving a Tsunami — Lessons from Chile, Hawaii and Japan', *U.S. Geological Survey Circular*, 1187 Version 1.1 (2005) gives details about the 1960 Chile tsunami. A *Reuters Alertnet* story from October 28, 2009 'How the Indian Ocean Tsunami Warning System Works' contained the statistic about phone numbers from nations' warning centers (www.alertnet.org/db/an_art/59567/2009/09/28-122125-1.htm).

Information about the inner-workings of the German-built system comes from Fauzi, Jorn Behrens, and GITEWS literature. Feedback on its shortcomings comes from tsunami scientists around the world.

'Surviving a Tsunami' also describes the reactions to the tsunami warning in Hilo in 1960. *The Science and Development Network* ran a story on January 25, 2010, 'Tsunami Alerts Must be Tailored to People, Says Report', that lays out the basic shortcomings from warning systems in the Indian Ocean, including the malfunctioning buoys (www.scidev.net/en/news/tsunami-alerts-must-be-tailored-to-people-says-report.html).

Losses in Thailand and their impact on tourism come from a variety of sources, including 'Investigator Will Not Release Tsunami Probe Findings: Report', *Agence France Press*, Bangkok, March 9, 2005; from 'Thailand Conducts Tsunami Evacuation Drill, Hoping to Draw Back Tourists', *Associated Press Newswires*, Bangkok, July 25, 2007; and from 'Thailand: Final Confirmed Numbers of Tourists in Phuket During 2005 Show Disappointing Outcome', *Thai News Service*, May 25, 2006. Tourism's piece of the Thai economy comes from the Library of Congress, Federal Research Division Country Profile on Thailand, July 2007.

The experiences in Thailand warnings come from Thomalla, Frank, et. al. 'From Knowledge to Action: Learning to Go the Last Mile',

Swedish Environment Institute, 2009 and Thomalla, et. al. 'Disaster Risk Reduction and Tsunami Early Warning Systems in Thailand: A Case Study on Krabi Province', *Swedish Environment Institute*, 2009 (www. sei-international.org).

10.

GTZ's survey after the September 30, 2009 earthquake '30 Minutes in Padang' is at www.gitews.org.

The Earthquake Engineer Research Institute put together a special report 'Learning from Earthquakes: The Mw 7.6 Western Sumatra Earthquake of September 30, 2009' on the engineering issues that led to so much collapse (www.eqclearinghouse.org/20090930-padang). Veronica Cedillos and Gregory Deierlein explained the findings in depth.

Several students and relatives in Padang spoke of the cracks at STBA Prayoga and their wariness about the place. One said he'd left for good after 2007.

The trail of John McCloskey's pronouncement picks up in London in 'The September 2009 Padang Earthquake', *Nature Geoscience* Vol. 3, February 2010, pp. 70–71, then goes to Paris in 'Tsunami-Generating Quake Possible off Indonesia: Scientists' by Richard Ingham in *Agence France Presse*, January 16, 2010, then out to the world. The website *detik.com* was one Indonesian outlet that tried to translate the story, which is where the word 'prediction' crept in to characterize his 2005 forecast before Nias. (www.us.detiknews.com/read/2010/01/18/104 942/1280520/10/gempa-tsunami-dahsyat-berpotensi-terjadi-lagi-di-sumatera?881103605). The *Padang Ekspres* story is only in hard copy at the moment.

Updates on the progress in West Sumatra one year after the quake came from *The Jakarta Globe* (www.thejakartaglobe.com/indonesia/ quake-city-bounces-back-stronger-one-year-on/398807) and *Al Jazeera* (www.youtube.com/watch?v=c7uCi1SYObY), and *The Jakarta Post* (www.thejakartapost.com/news/2010/09/29/new-site-focuses-quakeproof-homes.html).

Afterword

On sea level rise, see the Earth Observatory of Singapore's 'Starving Tigers: Impact of Climate Change in South East Asia' report published in January 2010 (www.rsis.edu.sg/nts/Events/Docs/EOS_Report_080710.pdf) and the article 'Sea Level Rise Could Bust IPCC Estimate' in the *New Scientist*, March 10, 2009 (www.newscientist.com/article/dn16732-sea-level-rise-could-bust-ipcc-estimate.html).

Thailand's rice challenges were studied in Felkner, et. al. 'Impact of Climate Change on Rice Production in Thailand', *American Economic Review*, 99 (2009): pp. 205–210 (www.hdl.handle.net/1721.1/51995).

Singapore's floods were reported by *Agence France Presse* in 'Flash Floods Stain Singapore's Reputation as Urban Paradise', July 18, 2010, and by two articles in *The Straits Times*: 'Insurance Costs May Rise with Flood Waters; Industry Reviewing Exposure in Flood-Prone Areas after Recent Events', July 23, 2010, and 'Floods Unavoidable: MM' by Jeremy Au Yong, July 21, 2010.

Many reporters interviewed Tilly Smith. One example is in 'Girl, 10, Used Geography Lesson to Save Lives', *The Telegraph* (U.K.) January 1, 2005 (www.telegraph.co.uk/news/1480192/Girl-10-used-geography-lesson-to-save-lives.html).

Further Reading

Alverson, Keith. 'Watching over the World's Oceans', *Nature,* Vol. 434 March 2005, pp. 19–20.

Atwater, Brian et. al. *The Orphan Tsunami of 1700.* Seattle: University of Washington Press and United States Geological Society, 2005.

Baker, Laurens. 'Tiele! Turis! The Social and Ethnic Impact of Tourism in Siberut (Mentawai)'. Unpublished MA thesis in Cultural Anthropology, Leiden University, The Netherlands, 1999.

Berak, Barry. 'The Day the Sea Came'. *New York Times Magazine,* Nov. 27, 2005.

Boomgaard, Peter. 'Crisis Mortality in Seventeenth Century Indonesia' in *Asian Population History,* ed. Ts'ui-jung Liu et. al. New York: Oxford University Press, 2001.

Bourne, Joel K. 'New Orleans: A Perilous Future', *National Geographic,* August 2007, pp. 32–67.

Cashman, K. V. and S. J. Cronin. 'Welcoming a monster to the world: Myths, oral tradition, and modern societal response to volcanic disasters', *Journal of Volcanology and Geothermal Research,* 176 (2008), pp. 407–418.

Chlieh, M. et. al. 'Heterogeneous coupling of the Sumatran megathrust constrained by geodetic and paleogeodetic measurements', *Journal of Geophysical Research,* Vol. 113 (2007) B05305.

'The Day That Shook the World', NOVA telecast, March 29, 2005 www.pbs.org/wgbh/nova/transcripts/3208_tsunami.html.

Diamond, Jared. *Collapse: How Societies Choose to Fail or Succeed.* New York: Viking, 2005.

Dobbin, Christine. *Islamic Revival in a Changing Peasant Economy.* London and Malmo: Curzon Press, 1983.

Elegant, Simon. 'Living on a Fault Line', *TIME Asia*, Vol. 166, No. 25, December 19, 2005.

'Extra sensory perception', *Economist,* 01/06/2001, pp. 74–75.

Ferguson, James. 'The Tragedy of St. Pierre'. *Geographical,* May 2002, pp. 14–19.

Fischetti, Mark. 'Drowning New Orleans', *Scientific American,* October 2001, pp. 76–85.

Friend, Theodore. *Indonesian Destinies.* Cambridge, Mass.: Harvard University Press, 2003.

Hadler, Jeffrey. *Muslims and Matriarchs: Cultural Resilience in Indonesia Through Jihad and Colonialism.* Ithaca: Cornell University Press, 2008.

Huxley, John. 'Fear Fever', *Sydney Morning Herald,* May 2, 2009 News/Review p. 1.

Hyogo Framework for Action 2005–2015: Building the Resilience of Nations and Communities to Disasters from the World Conference on Disaster Reduction, Kobe, Hyogo, Japan January 18–22, 2005, available at unisdr.org.

Jankaew, Kruawun, et. al. 'Medieval forewarning of the 2004 Indian Ocean tsunami in Thailand', *Nature,* Vol. 455, October 30, 2008.

Kennedy, Jim et. al. 'The Meaning of 'Build Back Better': Evidence From Post-Tsunami Aceh and Sri Lanka', *Journal of Contingencies and Crisis Management,* Vol. 16 No. 1 March 2008, pp. 24–36.

Marsden, William. *The History of Sumatra.* 3rd Ed. Kuala Lumpur: Oxford University Press, 1966.

McAdoo, Brian G. et. al. 'Smong: How an oral history saved thousands on Indonesia's Simeulue Island during the December 2004 and March 2005 tsunamis', *Earthquake Spectra,* Volume 22, No. S3, pp. S661–S669, June 2006.

McPhee, John. *Assembling California.* New York: Farrar, Straus & Giroux, 1994.

McPhee, John. *The Control of Nature.* New York: Farrar, Straus & Giroux, 1990.

Memoir of the Life and Public Services of Sir Thomas Stamford Raffles, by his widow, Vol. 1. London: James Duncan, 1835.

Mingle, Jonathan. 'In Surprising Ways, A Himalayan Village Adapts to Climate Change', *Boston Globe* November 29, 2009, www.boston. com/bostonglobe/ideas/articles/2009/11/29/when_the_glacier_ left/

Nalbant, S., Steacy, S., Sieh, K., Natawidjaja, D. & McCloskey, J. 'Earthquake risk on the Sunda trench', *Nature,* 435, pp. 756–757.

Phillips, Nigel. *Sijobang: Sung Narrative Poetry of West Sumatra.* Cambridge: Cambridge University Press, 1981.

Reid, Anthony. *An Indonesian Frontier: Achenese and other Histories of Sumatra.* London: Oxford University Press, 2004.

Reid, Anthony, ed. *Witnesses to Sumatra: A Traveller's Anthology.* Kuala Lumpur: Oxford University Press, 1995.

Reid, Anthony, ed. *Verandah on Violence: The Background to the Aceh Problem.* Singapore: Singapore University Press, 2006.

Ricklefs, M.C. *A History of Modern Indonesia since c.1200*. Palo Alto, CA: Stanford, 2009.

Sanday, Peggy Reeves. *Women at the Center: Life in a Modern Matriarchy*. Ithaca: Cornell University Press, 2002.

Schefold, Reimar and Persoon, Gerard. 'Nature in songs, songs in nature: texts from Siberut, West Sumatra, Indonesia' from *Cultural and Spiritual Values of Biodiversity*, UNEP, 1999, pp. 105–112.

Sieh, Kerry. 'Sumatran Megathrust Earthquakes: From Science to Saving Lives', *Philosophical Transactions of the Royal Society*, 2006 #364, 1947–1963.

Stone, Richard. 'The Day the Land Tipped Over', *Science*, Vol. 314, No. 20 October 2006, pp. 406–409.

Sullivan, Walter. 'U.S., Japan and Russia Set Up Alarm System for Tidal Waves', *New York Times*, August 5, 1960, p. 1.

Swanson, Donald. 'Hawaiian oral tradition describes 400 years of volcanic activity at Klauea', *Journal of Volcanology and Geothermal Research*, Vol. 176 (2008), pp. 427–431

Wallace, Alfred Russel. *The Malay Archipelago*. London: Macmillan, 1869.

Wildavsky, Aaron and Dake, Karl. 'Theories of Risk Perception: Who Fears What and Why?', *Daedalus*, Vol. 119, No. 4 (Fall 1990), pp. 41–60.

Winchester, Simon. *Krakatoa*. New York: Harper Collins, 2003.

World Disasters Report: A Focus on Early Warning and Early Action 2009. International Federation of Red Cross and Red Crescent Societies, available at www.ifrc.org/publicat.

Index

About the Author

Oakley Brooks is an American journalist whose writing has appeared in newspapers and magazines around the world, including the *New York Times*, the *Los Angeles Times* and the *International Herald Tribune*. In 2009, he was writer-in-residence at the Earth Observatory of Singapore at Nanyang Technological University, among scientists  researching earthquakes, volcanoes, tsunamis and climate change. He now lives across the Ring of Fire in Portland, Oregon.